RAMANA MAHARSHI'S PHILOSOPHY OF EXISTENCE AND MODERN SCIENCE

The Convergence in their Vision of Reality

RAMANA MAHARSHI'S PHILOSOPHY OF EXISTENCE AND MODERN SCIENCE

The Convergence in their Vision of Reality

J. SITHAMPARANATHAN

MOTILAL BANARSIDASS PUBLISHERS
PRIVATE LIMITED • DELHI

First Edition : Delhi 2008

© J. Sithamparanathan, 2008

ISBN: 978-81-208-3298-5

MOTILAL BANARSIDASS
41 U.A. Bungalow Road, Jawahar Nagar, Delhi 110 007
8 Mahalaxmi Chamber, 22 Bhulabhai Desai Road, Mumbai 400 026
203 Royapettah High Road, Mylapore, Chennai 600 004
236, 9th Main III Block, Jayanagar, Bangalore 560 011
Sanas Plaza, 1302 Baji Rao Road, Pune 411 002
8 Camac Street, Kolkata 700 017
Ashok Rajpath, Patna 800 004
Chowk, Varanasi 221 001

PRINTED IN INDIA
By Jainendra Prakash Jain at Shri Jainendra Press,
A-45 Naraina, Phase-I, New Delhi 110 028
and published by Narendra Prakash Jain for
Motilal Banarsidass Publishers Private Limited,
Bungalow Road, Delhi 110 007

CONTENTS

Foreword vii

Acknowledgements xiii

INTRODUCTION 1

1. BEYOND MECHANISTIC PHYSICS 17
2. THE ONENESS OF THE UNIVERSE 29
3. THE UNREALITY OF SPACE AND TIME 57
4. THE UNIVERSE AND REALITY 69
5. THE VOID, FORM AND THE COSMIC DANCE 91
6. PATTERNS IN STRUCTURE AND CHANGE 101
7. A SELF-CONSISTENT UNIVERSE 124
8. THE NEW ORDER 153
9. THE PATH TO TRUTH 169

References 198

Recommended Reading 201

Index 203

Foreword

The dawn of the 21st century saw a definite shift in the conceptual framework within which scientific theories had hitherto been constructed. The process started in the last century. For several hundreds of years, the Western world had created a number of entrenched ideas and values.. Among them was the view that the Universe was a mechanical system composed of elementary building blocks. Even the human body was considered a machine. As such, in medicine, the procedure of replacement by body parts was introduced. It was presumed that life in society was a competitive struggle for existence. There was also the belief that unlimited material progress could be achieved through economic and technological growth. There was another belief that a society in which the female was subsumed under the male was a society that followed a basic law of nature. A radical revision of all these beliefs was fast taking place.

The new paradigm could be termed as a holistic world view where the world was now being seen as an integrated whole rather than a collection of disconnected parts. This view stressed and recognized the fundamental interdependence of all phenomena in this universe.

A philosophical school was founded by the Norwegian philosopher Arne Naess in the nineteen seventies in the last century where he distinguished between "shallow ecology" and "deep ecology". Shallow ecology was human centred. It viewed human beings as above or outside of Nature. Nature was only of "use" value to man. Deep ecology did not separate human beings or anything else in this wide world from their natural environment. Deep ecology viewed the world as a network of events that were fundamentally interconnected and interdependent. It recognized the intrinsic value of all living beings and placed humans as just one particular strand in the web of life.

This deep ecology concept is the emerging new vision of reality in the scientific world today and is consistent with the spiritual traditions of the Sanathana Dharma (perennial philosophy). Deep ecology asked profound questions about the very foundations of our modern way of life. It questioned the modern scientific and industrial viewpoints. It questioned the materialistic world view and way of life. It questioned the dominator system of social organization where patriarchy, imperialism, capitalism and racism hitherto ruled the roost.

Such questioning led to shifts in perceptions and ways of thinking too. Values started changing. From self assertion, the shift in thinking was towards integration. The Western industrial culture, for example, had been over-emphasizing the self assertive side and had neglected the integrative tendencies. The earlier viewpoint favoured competition, expansion and domination generally attributed to the male of the species. The new way of life favoured a shift in social organizations based on domination, which created hierarchies, towards networks and integration. Social organizations which earlier doled out finances for appropriate poverty alleviation projects started thinking in terms of assisting the poor to stand on their own feet. Scientist authors such as Dr. Fritjof Capra gave form to a uniform view of mind, matter and life.

Interdependence and interconnectedness had been stressed by religions from time immemorial, long before science took centre stage two or three centuries ago. It had been the view of enlightened religions that each human being was a marvellous creation with unlimited potential for evolution and not simply an isolated physical, biological, psychological phenomenon destined to exist in ignorance. We are each born with a wholeness said the Vedas. We are not fragments of the totality, a chip of the cosmos, but each of us is a full and miniature cosmos.

Om Puurnamadah Puurnamidam
Puurnaat Puurnamudachyate
Puurnasya Puurnamaadaaya
Puurnameva Avashishyate
Om Shanti Shanti Shanti

That is full and complete
This is full and complete
From fulness came out this fulness
When this fulness is taken out, what remains is also fulness
May there be peace at all times.

Unfortunately we have not been educated into wholeness. We have been trained only in separation (I and not I), competition (I am better; he is lesser) and isolation (what can I do?). We have been uprooted early in our lives from wholeness. As a result we have developed much psychological instability. We have become experts in lop sided growth, but are still novices in evolving as whole human beings. On the one hand, we have inherited bountiful off-products of technological advancement. But on the other, as human beings we remain unfulfilled, uncertain who we are, what we are, and insecure about our survival.

Great sages like Ramana Maharshi saw our pathetic state. He had seen his predicament but been able to transcend his isolation, separation and competitive spirit. He had been able to live in that wholeness which had a "wondrous vibrancy of harmony and rhythm, the sharp clarity of pure intelligence, the magnetism of love and compassion (and) the spontaneous flow of creativity" to quote Vimala Thakar of Mt. Abu in Rajasthan, India.

Awareness of the whole, while dealing with the particular, cannot be an art to be cultivated through academic study.

Awareness must become an actuality. It must be lived. Ramana Maharshi taught the simple practical discipline called "self enquiry" to transcend the limitations of the "Ego". "Knowing the Self, God is known" said Raman Maharshi. Without looking extraneously, Ramana wanted us to look inwards to understand the inside as well as the outside.

In Talk Number 112, Ramana had said "God is 'all that is' plus the Being. The ego 'I' is individuality plus the Being. And the world is all perceived diversity plus the Being In all cases, the Being alone is real while 'all that is', the individuality and the diversity are unreal adjuncts. Reality is pure Being (without any adjuncts)."

If we look at this statement from the standpoint of any organized religion, the commonality among the various religious dimensions could be perceived. God is perceived by all theistic religions as "all that is". The different religions forget the extra characteristic that should be added on to "all that is" in order to make up God. That is the state of Being that Ramana spoke of. Every religion speaks of "all that is" from its own background and standpoint and hence they differ in nomenclature. The explanation of "all that is" by each religion may differ but Being stands as a common feature of God in all religions. Thus the choice of the philosophy of Ramana by the author to represent the religious standpoint appears appropriate.

"Images of God" as Ramana says "are merely symbols of That which lies beyond all forms - the Reality." Modern physics states that the concepts we use to describe and understand Nature are limited. They are not features of Reality but mere creations of the human mind.

Modern physics and Eastern mysticism have been concerned with phenomena beyond the realm of sensory experience and in recent times Science and Eastern mysticism have arrived at the conclusion that our perceptions of reality are merely conceptual and are not the true nature of reality.

Foreword

This recent addition to the scientific cum mystical literature of the world by the author very elaborately and lucidly sets out the viewpoints of Science and Eastern mysticism to drive home the idea that there appears to be convergence of views between them in their Vision of Reality. Ramana Maharshi, the enlightened sage, having been someone who had lived in recent times, the author has chosen him as the ideal representative of the votaries of the perennial truth - Sanathana Dharma.

I must congratulate the author on his magnum opus which will be popular among scientifically minded moderners who would still like to view religion and mysticism through the tinted glasses of science. Yet, the conclusion of the author is that no more should the glasses be tinted. The taint of science seems to fade away. Science and Eastern mysticism have begun to view Reality with similar ordinary spectacles.

Justice C.V. Wigneswaran

Acknowledgements

The presentation of the recent advances in physics that have led to the world vision of modern science converging on that of Eastern mysticism has depended almost exclusively on material from Fritjof Capra's classic "The Tao of Physics". The presentation of Ramana Maharshi's philosophy and teachings has similarly drawn heavily on two books viz. "Talks with Sri Ramana Maharshi" by Munagala Venkataramiah and "Guru Vachaka Kovai" by Sri Muruganar. The debt to these sources is gratefully acknowledged.

Acknowledgement is also due to Mr. Clive Roberts for his meticulous proof reading and other improvements to the book, and above all for his efforts which have resulted in the publication of the book. Also to Mr. S.E. Narthana for his invaluable assistance in the preparation of the final manuscript.

INTRODUCTION

This book is addressed to two groups of readers. In the first are those, particularly with a Western background, who - disillusioned with materialism and feeling vaguely that there is something beyond - are in search of a philosophy of life that provides a vision of the true reality, and at the same time is in harmony with the findings of science. In the second group are those with an Eastern background, who - despite being the inheritors of such a philosophy - have tended to reject their precious inheritance, on the mistaken assumption that it is inconsistent with rationalism and the evidence of science.

The book explores the parallels and points of convergence between the new worldview of modern science on the one hand, and that which has *always* been held by most Eastern spiritual philosophies on the other. There have been other books on the subject. The unique feature of this one is that the points of convergence are set against the background of the teaching of Sri Ramana Maharshi, the greatest sage of recent times.

Eastern spiritual philosophy, especially as taught by Sri Ramana Maharshi, does not conflict with the essential doctrines of any other religion. It is hoped that after reading this book, readers - irrespective of religion - will look for and discern the esoteric meanings of their beliefs i.e. their deeper significance. In doing so, the hitherto treasured but divisive outer 'shells' - mainly comprising various historical and cultural traditions - will not be confused with the essence of their religion. They will arrive at the essential teaching that forms the common ground underlying all religions. *When the unity of all religions is thus recognized, the accretions of the different religions will then contribute to a richness of religious diversity, not to religious discord.*

Beginning around the middle of the 18th century, the successes of western science led to its being invested with an aura of truth and infallibility. This attitude, which arose in the developed Western countries, has now spread among the educated and influential upper classes in the poorer developing countries. The Eastern spiritual philosophies have simultaneously been denigrated as being irrelevant to practical life. Science was considered to have demolished these philosophies and reduced them either to unfounded speculation or superstition.

Physics is the basis of all the natural sciences since the aim of physics, ever since the first period of Greek philosophy around the sixth century B.C., has been to discover the 'physis' or essential nature of all things. In contrast to Western theology, this has also been the central aim of most Eastern spiritual thought. *It is therefore of profound significance to those in search of the truth regarding the essential nature of the world that, far from demolishing the teachings of the Eastern spiritual philosophies, recent advances in physics have actually tended to confirm and substantiate them in scientific terms.* Eastern spiritual thought has thus been revealed to be closer to the truth regarding the universe than the theories of classical science!

The first chapter in the book presents a brief overview of the historical development of physics Subsequent chapters present in-depth explorations of the revolutionary concepts that have emerged in modern physics. All of them have tended to undermine those associated with conventional scientific wisdom and moved the scientific worldview in the direction of the Eastern spiritual philosophies. *Western philosophy, which provided classical physics with its philosophical basis, no longer does so for the modern science. Its philosophical basis is now provided by the Eastern spiritual philosophies!*

Modern physics has now arrived at a worldview that views the universe as an indivisible and undifferentiated unity - a dance of energy. It no longer regards the universe as a regulated mechanical system comprising separate, solid and independent elementary components, as envisaged in classical physics. Among the other new concepts that have emerged in modern physics and resulted in a revolutionary change in the scientific worldview are: the picture of matter as dynamic energy patterns rather than inanimate, tiny, indestructible, solid particles; the equivalence of both force and matter because of their common origin in these dynamic energy patterns; and the illusory nature of space, time, causation and opposites - from the standpoint of the multi-dimensional reality that underlies the universe. Perhaps even more significant, and bringing the scientific worldview even closer to the Eastern spiritual philosophies, are the more recent discoveries that - since the universe is a web of relations including the observer - an objective description of nature is impossible; that all concepts are creations of the human mind guided by sensory perception, and therefore transcended when one moves beyond them; that matter does not exist as such but only shows tendencies to exist; and that the real basis of the universe is a void or boundless energy field from and into which the particles that constitute material phenomena materialize and vanish. Forms are seen merely as manifestations of a cosmic 'Consciousness-Energy' principle. This is almost identical with the position held by most Eastern spiritual philosophies, which hold that all things, beings and events are transient, ever-changing and illusory manifestations of, and in, an underlying unity and reality of the nature of 'Existence-Consciousness'.

There are several spiritual philosophies in the East. *Modern science shows the closest convergence only towards those among them that postulate an indivisible, undifferentiated and un-manifest unity as the sole reality, and regard the diversity of perceived forms merely as illusory manifestations of this reality.* In these spiritual philosophies, experiential knowledge of the un-manifest reality is categorized as absolute or higher knowledge, while knowledge of the manifest plurality - knowledge in the normal use of the term - is considered to be relative or lower knowledge. Instances of such philosophies are the Upanishads, which enshrine the philosophical content of the ancient Hindu scriptures known as the Vedas; Advaita Vedanta, which is a more recent and systematized non-dualistic philosophy developed by the great Indian spiritual philosopher Sankara; the Avatatamsaka Sutra produced by Indian religious genius; Mahayana Buddhism as developed by the sages Ashvaghosha and Nagarjuna; the Chinese Hua-yen school of Buddhism, which is an interpretation of the Avatamsaka Sutra in the light of Chinese philosophy; Chinese Taoist philosophy; and Zen Buddhism which combines the mysticism of India, Taoist naturalness and spontaneity and Confucian pragmatism.

In this book however, the timeless spiritual philosophy of the East, as expounded by Sri Ramana Maharshi, has been preferred. In the Maharshi's view, pre-occupation with doctrine and philosophical speculation was actually detrimental to the seeker of truth for two reasons. First, the reality or truth of the universe is such that it cannot ever be comprehended by the human mind It can only be known through direct intuitive experience. Second, getting bogged down in doctrine and philosophical arguments distracted the seeker of truth from the really important task of realizing it directly through such experience. *Maharshi's exposition is therefore characterized by a minimum of complex, confusing, philosophical speculation aimed at satisfying the interminable questioning of the mind. Instead, it presents the seeker with a simple, undiluted and authoritative exposition of his direct mystical insight into the nature of the ultimate reality.* It is also *scientific in its approach since it describes and emphasizes direct and less direct approaches by which the truth of such insight can be realized.* If listened to, tentatively accepted - as we do with scientifically demonstrated facts - and then reflected upon, it launches the seeker on a quest to experience its truth for oneself. *Much of spiritual philosophy and religion - both in the East and in the West - is however a diluted or degraded interpretation of true mystic insight or revelation, designed by minds to satisfy the mind.* Whereas their real purpose should be to serve as a bridge to help the sincere seeker cross from belief in the superficial falsity of the world appearance to its underlying truth, most philosophies have tended to degenerate into dogma or doctrine. Rather than help him cross from illusion to reality, they build a house on the bridge for him to admire and live in.

Maharshi's Teaching

The essence of Maharshi's teaching is that it is the human mind alone that is the main obstacle to our realizing the truth or reality. It must therefore be transcended if one is to arrive at the truth. Seeking the truth through the aid of the mind was like seeking the help of the thief to recover what he has stolen. The analogy is apt since, according to the Maharshi, it is the mind that has 'stolen' or deprived us of awareness of our true nature and that of the world Remarkably, *science now substantiates this teaching, having come to the conclusion that all concepts are merely mental constructs; they are maps, not the territory; that what we perceive is merely a sensory impression of reality; and that the mind can never arrive at the reality underlying the perceived universe.*

Another reason for selecting the teachings of Maharshi as the best presentation of Eastern spiritual philosophies is that *it is a clear and uncompromising exposition of the direct mystic insight of a sage in the twentieth century - recorded in his very words. Being so recent, there has been no room for the inevitable distortions and dilutions of an original teaching or revelation that tend to occur as a result of interpretation and re-interpretation* by successive generations of mere scholars, clerics and philosophers. For these reasons, its content comes closest in its essence to that of the Upanishads - the perennial philosophy and wellspring of almost all other Eastern spiritual philosophies.

Maharshi's exposition of his mystic insight into reality is closely linked to a simple practical spiritual discipline that he called 'self enquiry'. If practised with single-minded resolve, it leads one to secure, for oneself, the same mystic insight into the essential nature of the truth or absolute reality underlying the universe. There is here a close parallel to the teaching of natural science, where a student is first taught factual knowledge derived from research, and then the experimental procedure by which he can verify it for himself. *To the Maharshi, intellectual comprehension of his philosophy - the verbal expression of his insight into the nature of reality - was necessary only to the extent of convincing oneself that it pointed towards the absolute truth. Thereafter, all effort was to be directed towards gaining the mystic experience of truth for oneself.*

The spiritual discipline prescribed by the Maharshi for this purpose can be practiced by anyone, provided his or her present set of beliefs about the world are held merely as a tentative view rather than as a rigid dogma, and one is flexible, willing and humble enough to make a change when it seems warranted. This is the scientific attitude, and it has led science towards the truth behind Nature. *At every stage in its progress, science has been prepared to abandon concepts that it earlier regarded as sacrosanct. Such an attitude of mind is an equally essential pre-requisite for anyone seeking the ultimate truth or reality behind all beings and the physical world.*

In exploring the points of convergence between modern science and Eastern spiritual philosophy, the approach of the book (Chapters 2 to 7) has been to present, in relation to each point of convergence, some selected teachings of the Maharshi. These have been taken mainly from two books, *'Talks with Sri Ramana Maharshi'* and *'The Garland of Guru's Sayings'* In the first book, conversations between the Maharshi and devotees were faithfully recorded. For the sake of brevity, many of the quotations from this book represent abbreviated versions of what was actually recorded, but the meaning has not been altered. The number of the relevant Talk is given against each quotation so that, in case of doubt, its correctness may be verified. This prevents the possibility of distortion in the presentation of his philosophy and teachings.

It is hoped that the presentation of the Maharshi's teachings in this manner will encourage *repeated reflection upon them in the context of their convergence with the findings of modern science.* With repeated reflection, more esoteric or deeper meanings of the more cryptic quotations will be discerned. It is as if they emerge only when the seeker is ready to receive them. The main purpose of the book is indeed to promote such reflection, so that it may lead eventually to a firm intuitive conviction of their truth.

In the absence of such conviction, those of us who rigidly cling to the (now outmoded) Cartesian 'compartmentalizing' scientific temper are unlikely to allow the philosophy to influence our lives, and to open ourselves to what should be the highest purpose of our earthly existence viz. the practice of a spiritual discipline that will lead us to a direct experience of the one Reality behind all the things, beings and activities of the universe. *If science is the search for the ultimate truth, the quest for such an experience of the ultimate reality has greater claim to being a scientific enterprise, in the truest sense of the term, than much of today's much vaunted 'scientific' research, which is more in the nature of technology development in the service of mankind's superficial and baser aims.*

The human being has two sides to his nature viz. the subtler spiritual side and the gross, physical or material side. Hence the saying *'Man does not live by bread alone'*. Complete acceptance of the worldview of 'classical' science and the consequent rejection of all spiritual philosophy - on the ground that it has been debunked by science - has resulted over the past two centuries in the spiritual side of one's existence being almost completely eclipsed by the physical side. By drawing one's attention to the subtle spiritual aspect of one's individual existence and that of the world, and emphasizing the fundamental nature of the spiritual relative to the gross material aspect - in terms that are suited to the current scientific age - *the Maharshi's philosophy helps one to achieve a proper balance between the two sides of one's nature.* One is enabled to live both in the more fundamental and inner world of the spirit, as well as in the outer material world. Abiding in and anchored in the former i.e. in one's true nature as spirit, one gains the wisdom to live and act in the latter, in peace, harmony and serenity.

Maharshi's philosophy is of value to us at two levels. At the higher, it offers those with a more strongly developed spiritual nature and a sincere yearning for the truth, a spiritual philosophy and a path that will lead them to direct intuitive experience of the Truth or Reality. At the lower, it provides guiding principles and values for those who merely wish to lead a happier, more harmonious and serene life at the mundane level of material existence. Pointing out that all opposites (including right and wrong, good and evil) are not contrasting distinct entities but complementary aspects of the same ultimate reality, the *Maharshi's philosophy of non-duality defines right conduct, not merely as moral eschewing of wrong and evil, but as the turning of one's mind inwards,* so that one approaches and finally abides permanently in one's true and perfect nature. Christ's injunction *"Be ye perfect as thy Father in heaven is perfect"* is an expression of this spiritual philosophy.

The philosophy also provides us with a rational basis for freedom from fear, desires and passions. As all beings and the universe are declared to be one with the infinite, eternal Being-Awareness that is the sole reality and immanent in them, there can be no 'other' to be feared or desired. Acceptance of the principle of 'non-duality' therefore enables us to view all objects and events in worldly life with equanimity. Hence, the other aphorism of Christ *"Seek ye the truth for the truth shall make you free".*

Since our greatest love is for ourselves, the doctrine of non-duality - that all beings are, in essence, the one Self - provides a rational basis for love and compassion towards all other beings. This is the esoteric or deeper meaning of Christ's injunction *"Love thy neighbour as thy self"*. We are not individual and separate selves. There is only the one eternal and infinite Self that is immanent in all.

Acceptance of Maharshi's mystic vision that the universe and all beings therein are manifestations of an organic, indivisible and harmonious whole also demolishes our sense of individuality and the attendant arrogant and deluded notion that we have the power to determine the course of events. It rationalizes the faith enjoined by most Eastern religions that a divine power immanent in the universe works through us. It follows that surrender to the divine will is supreme wisdom. Christ taught a similar faith in divine guidance and power when he said that *"not even a sparrow can fall to the ground without the divine will; that the very hairs on one's head were numbered; and that one should not plan for the morrow"*. Recent advances in physics (presented in Chapter 7) have, remarkably, now provided a scientific foundation for this view. Surrender is not fatalism but grounded in a reality, similarly perceived both by mystics and physicists.

Maharshi's philosophy states that our true nature is immortal, infinite and perfect; that our sense of mortality, finiteness and imperfection is a delusion born of identification with the ego or sense of individuality; and that this delusion can be overcome by transcending its cause (the illusory ego). It is only so long as we allow the ego sense - the 'I' thought - to govern our lives that we allow ourselves to be estranged from our true divine nature. *Our true nature is the unbroken, unalloyed bliss of Pure Consciousness.* We alienate ourselves from the blissful and perfect reality that we truly are and lose ourselves in the transient pleasures and sorrows of an illusory world. But Maharshi shows us a way whereby *we can, even in this life, regain and abide in our true nature as Existence-Consciousness-Bliss.* Such a philosophy surely has a greater appeal and offers greater hope and purpose to mankind than *any worldview that regards our real nature as mortal, finite and imperfect. It provides us with a rational basis for regarding the transcending of the ego as one's highest aim in life.*

For this reason, Maharshi's philosophy elaborates on the nature of the ego; its expanded form, the mind; and the approach to overcoming them. The finite outward looking mind, born of the ego and made up of thought, is a veil that masks our true immortal, infinite and perfect nature from us. As it thrives on attention to its own creation, the world, one is directed to turn one's attention or awareness inwards, away from attachments to the world. This is perhaps the esoteric significance of the Christ's statement *"Get thee behind me, Satan"*. Starved of attention, the hold of the ego sense is weakened and it finally vanishes. Once it is vanquished, one's true divine nature stands revealed. *Maharshi has offered the discipline of 'self enquiry' as the most direct means of overcoming the ego, and indicated rationally and scientifically why it alone can directly lead to success. None of the other spiritual disciplines is denigrated, but it is explained why they are merely steps on the way, and must all eventually lead to the path of self-enquiry.*

The path of devotion to a personal anthropomorphic God - which is emphasized in the dualistic religions - was accepted by the Maharshi as being appropriate for those whose temperament precluded them from following the direct path of self-enquiry. But *devotion, in his philosophy, meant aspiring towards the complete surrender of one's sense of individuality,* - not mere adoration of, and service to, the God of one's faith in a permanent subject-object relationship. The absence of open expression of non-duality in these religions is, in itself, not a great disadvantage since the devotional path leads to mystic union. From this point, divine grace - requiring no personal effort - merges the soul in the One, the Formless Absolute. *The unfortunate shortcoming in these religions is the ignorance or outright denial of the possibility of non-duality and its corollary, the possibility of man's attaining to perfection. But Christ himself proclaimed this possibility.*

"Be ye perfect as thy Father in heaven is perfect."

Modern science and Eastern spirituality now concur that the universe and all beings therein are merely manifestations of, in, and by a dynamic, integral and universal Consciousness. Intellectual acceptance of this truth makes possible a change in one's approach to worldly life. It becomes rational to move away from an outlook based on the illusion of separateness; subjection to desires and passions; and the false notion that one really has personal control over one's activities and Nature. Instead, one adopts an outlook that bases one's actions on an understanding of the indivisible unity and harmony of all existence; that makes equanimity in the face of pleasures and sorrows possible; and accepts that one is - as participant - subject to the inexorable laws inherent in nature.

At the time of the Renaissance, Western civilization abandoned its religious foundation and adopted rationalism, science and humanism as its basis. From being theocentric, it became anthropocentric. Several centuries later, it has found its fulfilment in a secular and mechanized society where materialist and utilitarian values dominate. The spiritual basis of life remains as a sort of secret treasure for those who refuse to go with the tide. Eastern nations too have, over the past century begun to succumb to this trend towards spiritual degeneracy, - rapidly abandoning the spiritual basis of their life and culture.

In the secular nation state, spiritual values and interests are completely subordinated to the secular. By removing education, law, government and the whole organization of life from the influence of spiritual values, it has reduced religion and spiritual values to little more than personal faith or private opinion. Social service is deemed the truest religion, while mysticism and renunciation are denigrated as anti-social. This is natural in a materialist society that exalts man's powers and ignores or denies the existence of any superior power.

In Chapter 8, it is shown that *the crisis facing the world today - in the form of a host of social, economic, environmental and political problems - may be traced to the dominance of the rationalist approach to worldly life.* The problems are the result of a web of relationships created through over-emphasis on the values and attitudes associated with rationalism, to the near exclusion of those based on intuition. Both modern science and Eastern spirituality however now concur that it is the dynamic balance between opposites that is the basis of harmony and stability in the unceasing cosmic process. It therefore justifies the thesis that, *in the behaviour of individuals and society too, there is a need to balance the values and attitudes associated with both rationalism and intuition - the secular and the spiritual - if harmony and stability are to prevail.*

The social, economic and political institutions of the purely secular state may therefore need to be restructured. Modern systems theory provides a scientific, as well as spiritual, basis for such restructuring, since it looks at organisms, societies and ecosystems as *living* systems, - as wholes within which all sub-systems and phenomena are intimately inter-related and interdependent. Both modern science and mysticism now recognize the unity of the universe, and the consequent complementarity of opposites within living systems. *The health of the system thus depends on a balance or dynamic interplay between properties associated with the two polar i.e. opposite but complementary, tendencies of self-assertion and integration.* Each part or sub-system must assert its individuality in order to maintain the system's stratified order, but it must also submit to the demands of the whole in order to make the system viable.

The self-assertive tendency is associated with rational, analytic, expansionary, aggressive and competitive behaviour. The integrative tendency is, on the other hand, associated with behaviour that is intuitive, synthesizing, contractionary, responsive and co-operative. *That there is excessive aggression in so-called 'modern' society is manifested in the fact that power, control and forcible domination of others are its major features.* There is increasing dominance by a dominant corporate class; repression of minorities; plunder of the earth's finite natural resources; and domination rather than participation in nature. Technology is aimed at control and mass production, - directed by centralized management that pursues the illusory and unnatural goal of indefinite growth.

Promotion of competitive rather than co-operative behaviour is the other significant manifestation of the self-assertive tendency. Competition is seen and promoted as the driving force behind the economy. An 'aggressive approach' is the ideal of the business world and, in combination with the ideal of unlimited and competitive consumption, has resulted in a continuing and indiscriminate exploitation of finite natural resources.

If our world is to resolve its manifold problems and recover its stability and harmony, the self-assertive tendency must be balanced by greater emphasis on the integrative tendency. The values and behavioural characteristics associated with this tendency must find a greater place in our social, economic and political institutions. Among other things, this implies a shift from 'macho' to 'soft' technologies; scaling down of enterprises and institutions; movement away from material consumption to voluntary simplicity; a greater concern for the environment arising from a sense of being a participant therein; and, above all, movement away from obsession with economic and technological growth towards a greater concern for inner growth and development. *There is, in short, a need for adoption of values based on Eastern spiritual philosophy, to restore the balance between the two tendencies of self-assertion and integration in all aspects of our social, cultural and economic life.* By providing a scientific basis for the spiritual argument for such a development, modern physics has made it much easier to bring about such a change in the values and attitudes of our science dominated society. At last, science and spirituality can lead the world, hand in hand, towards a better world.

When my book on ecology and a holistic approach to agriculture was published in 2001, I had no inkling whatsoever that I would soon embark upon another book. Inexplicably however the idea of writing this book arose, and simultaneously the guidance to do so also seemed to come out of nowhere. Often I had only to wish for clarification on some particular point and a book providing it would turn up! Science and spiritual philosophy are now in agreement that all events fit perfectly into a pre-ordained scheme of things, and that we are therefore mere agents of the divine will. The circumstances surrounding the writing of this book have confirmed my belief that it is really so. No personal authorship is therefore claimed for the book. The creator of the book is, to me the author, the Great Doer

The explosion in communications technology is presently being used to flood the public with much information that does little to help mankind to turn inwards, find serenity and happiness within, and lead a life in harmony with nature. *There is no defence against drowning in this flood of largely useless information in the absence of an authoritative, credible and proven vision of the true nature of the universe, of ourselves and the highest ideal in life. The spiritual philosophy taught by Sri Ramana Maharshi provides us with just such a vision, especially as it has largely been corroborated by modern science.* Such a vision, and its associated value system, would help us discriminate between useless and useful information and not waste our valuable lives imbibing the former. Information technology will then not be another razor in the hands of a fool.

Introduction

Despite enjoying very high levels of affluence, amidst the abject poverty endured by the vast majority of the world's population, the rich nations of the world still pursue economic growth as their primary aim! Their view of the ancients is that they were primitive and without aspirations, to be satisfied with bare existence. All the older civilizations, however, extolled the virtues of simple and shared living; of contentment and spiritual satisfaction; and even renunciation. The question here is the sense of values adopted by individuals and society. What is the birthright and what is the mess of pottage? Anthropological studies have shown that the brain of man has not evolved in the slightest over the past ten thousand years. The case for linking the advances in science and technology development over the past three centuries with greater intelligence is thus demolished. The more logical explanation, which accords with recorded history, is that these advances - especially since the 18th century - have resulted from the progressive dominance of material values over those based on spiritualism, and the consequent diversion of human energies from spiritual to materialistic goals. It is only if people have always had the modern materialistic sense of values, that one can justify the view that lack of ability and initiative prevented the earlier great civilizations from creating the materially elaborate, possession oriented and mechanized civilization of today. *The ancients apparently based their civilizations on a higher (and wiser) sense of values, where more emphasis was laid on the spiritual. Modern man who has blinded himself to a higher sense of values can hardly be expected to credit the ancients with one!* The need today is to recover this higher sense of values - a proper balance of the spiritual and the material. Technological advances will then no longer fascinate us, feed our greed, and distract us from the great and rewarding adventure of realizing the bliss of our real divine state All religions are unanimous in declaring that excessive wealth and attachment are incompatible with spiritual progress and realization of this divine state - variously described as the Kingdom of God, Liberation, Self-realization or Bliss.

"It is easier for a camel to pass through the eye of the needle than for a rich man to enter the kingdom of God." (Jesus).

"Loss of attachments is the gain of Home (Liberation)." (Auvaiyar, Hindu saint-poetess).

CHAPTER 1

BEYOND MECHANISTIC PHYSICS

INTRODUCTION

The Western view of the world during the 18th and 19th centuries was based on the philosophy of Rene Descartes who saw Nature as comprising two separate and independent realms, viz. that of matter, and that of mind This spirit-matter dualism had led scientists to approach the subject of matter on the basis that it is inanimate, and regard the world of matter as akin to a regulated machine. Newtonian mechanics was founded on this philosophy and it became the foundation of classical physics Alongside, there was the spirit world with the image of God as a monarchical figure who ruled the world from above, through divine laws. Physicists saw their mission as the uncovering of these laws of God.

Up to the beginning of the 20th century, physicists made observations on phenomena in the realm of their sensory experience, or expanding such experience using relatively unsophisticated equipment. Intellectual concepts and images drawn from this very experience were therefore adequate to explain, to the rational mind, the phenomena being studied. From the beginning of the 20th century however, the highly sophisticated instruments of modern experimental physics enabled scientists to probe deeper into the sub-microscopic world beyond sensory experience, and uncover layer after layer in their search for the ultimate 'building blocks' of matter Thus, the existence of atoms, their nuclei and electrons, protons and neutrons and finally other sub-atomic particles, was discovered. These discoveries were made, not through sensory perception, but by 'observing' the properties of atoms and their invisible constituents in an indirect way. The existence of these constituents was deduced from observation of the consequences of their existence.

On this journey to the world of the infinitesimally small, science transcended the limits of imagination based on sensory experience. Knowledge of matter at this level is no longer derived from sensory experience and consequently ordinary language, which takes its images from the sensory world, is no longer adequate to describe the observed phenomena. Scientists were now dealing with non-sensory experience of reality, and from this time onwards the models and images of modern physics have approached those of Eastern religious philosophies.

CLASSICAL PHYSICS

The Newtonian Model

The Newtonian model of the universe had, as its stage, the 3-dimensional space of classical Euclidean geometry. It was absolute i.e. independent of anything external; always at rest, and unchanging. All changes in the physical world were described in terms of a separate dimension called time This was again absolute. It had no connection with the material world and it flowed smoothly from the past, through the present, into the future. The elements of the Newtonian world that moved in this absolute space and absolute time were material particles. All matter was made out of these tiny, solid and indestructible particles.

The particles were assumed to remain always identical in mass and shape. Matter was therefore always conserved, immutable and passive. The force of gravity, depending only on mass and distance, acted between these material particles. All physical events were reduced to the motion of material bodies in space, caused by their mutual attraction under the force of gravity. By his invention of differential calculus, Newton was able to formulate his equations pertaining to motion, as well as the laws according to which material particles move.

This purely mechanistic view of nature was closely linked to the concept of rigorous determinism. All that happened in the world had a definite cause, which gave rise to a definite effect. The philosophical basis for this determinism was the fundamental division between the 'I' and the world, postulated by Descartes. It was believed that the world could be described objectively i.e. without any reference to the observer. Such objective description of nature became the ideal of science.

Newton's mechanistic model had great success in explaining the mechanics of the solar system, the flow of the tides and other phenomena related to gravity, the theory of heat and the vibrations of elastic bodies. It led physicists to believe that the universe was indeed a huge mechanical system running according to the Newtonian laws of motion. These laws were seen as the basic laws of nature.

Electrodynamics

The limitations of the Newtonian model became apparent with the discovery and study of electrical and magnetic phenomena These phenomena showed that none of the features of the model had absolute validity. Faraday and Maxwell, by making these electric and magnetic forces the primary object of their research, formulated a complete theory of electromagnetism They also replaced the concept of 'force' by that of a 'force field'. A 'force field' was defined as a 'condition' in space that had the potential of producing a force. The significant point is that a 'force field' exists, whether or not its effect is felt as a force. By their work, they were the first to go beyond Newtonian physics because in the Newtonian view forces were rigidly connected with the bodies they acted upon. Now the concept of force was replaced by the much subtler concept of a 'force field' which had its own reality and could be studied without any reference to the material bodies they acted upon.

The culmination of the theory of 'force fields' - called electrodynamics - was the realization that light, radio waves and X-rays are rapidly alternating electromagnetic fields travelling through space in the form of waves. They differ only in the frequency of their oscillation Einstein was the first to recognize that electromagnetic fields were physical entities in their own right, which travelled through empty space and could not be explained mechanically. By the start of the 20th century, physics therefore had two very successful theories that applied to different sets of phenomena viz. Newtonian mechanics and Maxwell's electrodynamics.

MODERN PHYSICS

During the first three decades of the 20th century, relativity theory and quantum theory have shattered the principal concepts and foundations of the Newtonian world view viz. the notions of absolute space and time, elementary solid particles, the strictly causal nature of physical phenomena and the ideal of an objective description of nature. All these concepts did not apply in the new domains into which physics was moving.

The Special Theory of Relativity

The 'special theory of relativity' was the result of Einstein's effort to construct a common framework for electrodynamics and mechanics – the two separate themes of classical physics at the time. It unified and completed the structure of classical physics, but in the process it undermined the traditional concepts of absolute space and time.

Beyond Mechanistic Physics

According to relativity theory, space is not 3-dimensional, and time is not separate from space. Both are intimately connected to form a 4-dimensional continuum called 'space time'. There is also no universal flow of time i.e. different observers will perceive events differently in time, if their velocities of movement relative to the observed events are different. *Both space and time were thus reduced to mere elements of a language used by observers for describing observed phenomena.*

This revolutionary modification of the concepts of space and time entailed changing the entire framework used by scientists to describe nature. *The most important consequence was the realization that mass is nothing but a form of energy.* The relation between the two was given by Einstein's famous equation $E = mC^2$ The profound implication of this realization was that when scientists deal with physical phenomena involving velocities approaching that of light, they must take relativity theory into account. This applies specially to electromagnetic phenomena.

Einstein subsequently formulated his 'general theory of relativity' to include gravity Its revolutionary concept is that the gravitational field of massive bodies actually causes curvature of 3-dimensional space. And since space is inseparable from time in relativity theory, time is also affected by the presence of matter and flows differently in different parts of the universe. The classical concepts of space and time were therefore completely nullified. *Not only are all measurements of space and time relative but also the whole structure of 'space-time' depends on the distribution of matter in the universe.*

The mechanistic world view of classical physics – based on the notion of solid bodies moving in empty space – is nevertheless still valid in the realm of our daily experience, called the 'zone of middle dimensions'. It however does not apply when we go beyond this zone in either direction. *The concept of 'empty* space' has had to be abandoned in astrophysics and cosmology, which are the sciences of the universe at large; while the concept of solid matter has had to be similarly abandoned in the realm of atomic physics - which is the science of the infinitely small.

The Quantum Theory

The discovery of various types of radiation emitted by atoms was the first indication that atoms had some internal structure. By using alpha particles (which are high speed projectiles of sub-atomic size emanating from radioactive substances) Rutherford was able to demonstrate that atoms were not the hard and solid particles that they had been assumed to be, but vast regions of empty space in which extremely small particles (electrons) moved around a central nucleus – bound to it by electric forces. While the size of an atom is infinitely small, it is however huge compared to the nucleus at its centre. *Almost the whole of an atom therefore turned out to be space.*

The laws of atomic physics were discovered in the 1920s by an international group of physicists when they explored the strange and unexpected reality of the sub-atomic world. Attempts to describe sub-atomic structure and events in the terms of classical physics always resulted in paradoxes, until it was finally recognized that these paradoxes followed from the intrinsic nature of sub-atomic matter. They finally found precise and consistent formulation in the 'quantum theory', which made it clear that *the extremely small particles of the sub-atomic world were not solid, but very abstract entities, which also had a dual character. They appeared sometimes as particles and sometimes as waves.*

This dual character was also found to be exhibited by light, which can take the form of electromagnetic waves or particles. All electromagnetic radiation has now been shown to have this dual nature, appearing both as waves and as energy packets

Beyond Mechanistic Physics

known as 'quanta', which are mass-less and travelling at phenomenal velocities. This property of matter and also all electromagnetic radiation viz. to be, at the same time a particle (which is confined to a very small volume) and a wave (which is spread out over a very large region of space) was a paradox which gave rise to many others and was finally resolved by the formulation of 'quantum theory'

The quantum theory meant that the concept of the reality of matter had to be abandoned. At the sub-atomic level, matter does not exist with certainty at definite places, but rather shows 'tendencies to exist'. Correspondingly, atomic events are not occurrences that take place with certainty at definite times and in definite ways, but are rather in the nature of 'tendencies to occur'. In quantum theory these 'tendencies' relating to matter and events are expressed as 'probabilities' which are associated with mathematical quantities, which take the form of waves They are not real 3-dimensional waves like sound or water waves but abstract 'probability waves' They have all the properties of waves and relate to the probabilities of finding the particles at particular points in space at particular times. All the laws of atomic physics are expressed in terms of these probabilities.

Quantum theory has therefore demolished the classical concepts of solid matter and of strictly deterministic laws of nature. At the sub-atomic level, the solid matter of classical physics dissolves into wave like patterns of probabilities. These patterns do not represent probabilities in the concrete sense but rather probabilities of inter-connections. This is due to the fact that *sub-atomic particles have no meaning or reality as isolated entities but can only be understood as interconnections between the preparation of an experiment and the subsequent measurement.*

Quantum theory thus reveals a basic one-ness i.e. interconnectedness and indivisibility of the entire universe. It cannot be decomposed into independently existing smallest units in the nature of fundamental 'building blocks'. At the most fundamental level, matter turns out to be a complicated web of relations or inter-connections between various parts of the whole. Importantly, this web of relations also includes the observer in an essential way, since the human observer is the final link in the chain of observational processes. The observed properties of all atomic components can only be understood in terms of their interaction with the observer. *The classical ideal of an objective description of nature is therefore no longer valid, and the Cartesian division between observer and observed breaks down. We cannot speak about nature without, at the same time, speaking about ourselves.*

Quantum theory has been able to explain what makes matter feel solid to our touch despite the fact that the atoms of which they are composed consist almost entirely of empty space so far as the distribution of mass within them is concerned. In the atom, there are two distinct forces on the electrons. Electric forces binding them to the nucleus try to keep them as close as possible. The electrons respond to their confinement by whirling around at exceedingly high velocities of around 600 miles per second. *It is these high velocities that make the atom seem like a solid sphere. It is very difficult to compress atoms any further and hence the illusion of solidity.*

Quantum theory also explains the extraordinary mechanical stability of atoms. It is due to the wave nature of electrons. Because of their wave nature and their confinement to a finite region, the electron waves form patterns called 'standing waves' which can exist only in certain atomic orbits with specific diameters, and nowhere in between. In the atom, the electrons therefore settle in orbits in such a way that there is a perfect balance between the attraction of the nucleus and their reluctance to be confined. An electron can jump into a higher orbit if it receives the necessary quantum of energy, but it will go back to its usual orbit after a while by giving up the surplus energy in the form of electromagnetic radiation or photon. The atom is then said to be in its normal or 'ground state'. *Atoms are therefore extraordinarily stable mechanically despite colliding with others with a very high frequency, since they retain their characteristic configuration of electrons.*

The basic force which gives rise to all atomic phenomena is the force of electric attraction between the positively charged atomic nucleus and the negatively charged electrons. It is the interplay of this force with the electron waves that is responsible for all chemical reactions between atoms, and also the aggregation of atoms into molecules. It is thus the basis for the existence of all solids, liquids and gases, as well as all living organisms and their biological processes.

The atomic nuclei are extremely small but stable centres which constitute the source of the electric force. They also form the skeletons of the great variety of molecular structures since they contain practically all the mass Their two main constituents viz. the positively charged protons and electrically neutral neutrons, are very tightly held together within the nucleus by a phenomenally strong nuclear force. It is non-electromagnetic and not manifest anywhere outside the nucleus. This force is so strong that the density of matter inside the nucleus is infinitely greater than that of ordinary matter. The protons and neutrons respond to such a high degree of confinement by racing about within the nucleus at velocities of around 40,000 miles per second! *Nuclear matter is therefore a form of matter unimaginable in terms of our experience in the macroscopic world.*

Particle Physics

Relativity theory, as indicated earlier, showed that mass is not substance but a form of energy. Since energy is associated with activity or processes, the particle is now seen as a dynamic pattern or process involving the energy that manifests as the particle's mass. This dynamic, relativistic view of matter, which sees particles as dynamic patterns or processes, demolishes the classical view of matter as consisting of 'basic building blocks'. In a collision process, the energy of the two colliding particles is redistributed to form a new pattern rather than smaller particles. Thus collisions can occur resulting in the fragmentation of particles, but we do not end up with smaller fragments because new particles are created out of the energy involved in the collision process. *Sub-atomic particles are thus destructible and indestructible at the same time!*

Most of the particles created in collisions live only for an extremely short time - much less than a millionth of a second – after which they disintegrate. The particle world is thus dynamic and ever changing. Matter is therefore completely mutable. All particles can be transmuted into other particles. They can be created out of energy and vanish into energy. *The universe thus appears as a dynamic web of inseparable energy patterns!*

Particle physics has therefore revealed the basic unity and intrinsically dynamic nature of matter. The properties of a particle can only be understood in terms of its activity i.e. its interaction with the surrounding environment. *Particles cannot be regarded as isolated entities but rather as integrated parts of a whole.*

The forces between particles viz. their attraction or repulsion are also now conceived as the exchange of other particles. This concept springs from the 4-dimensional character of the sub-atomic world. *Both force and matter are now seen to have their common origin in the dynamic patterns that we call particles.*

The fact that particles interact through forces that manifest themselves as the exchange of other particles is yet another reason why the sub-atomic world cannot be regarded as made up of constituent building blocks. From the macroscopic level down to the nuclear level, the forces that hold things together are relatively weak, and it is a satisfactory approximation to speak of constituent parts. Thus we can speak of molecules comprising atoms; atoms comprising nuclei and electrons; and nuclei comprising protons and neutrons. But at the particle level it is no longer possible to see things in this way.

Protons and neutrons are composite in character, but the relativistic view of matter has to be applied here because the velocities of the forces holding them together are of the same magnitude as that of light. *In this relativistic view, forces are also particles; the distinction between constituent particles and the particles making up the binding forces becomes blurred; and the concept of an object comprising constituent particles is therefore no longer tenable. The particle world cannot be decomposed into elementary components.*

Modern physics therefore pictures the universe as a dynamic inseparable whole, which always includes the observer in an essential way. In this view, the traditional concepts which apply in the 'zone of middle dimensions' (the realm of sensory experience), such as absolute and independently existing space and time, matter as comprising basic 'building blocks', isolated physical entities, the solid nature of matter, cause and effect and the possibility of an objective description of nature, cease to have any meaning. Instead one deals with new and strange concepts such as a space-time continuum, mass as a form of energy, particles as dynamic energy patterns, matter as completely mutable, the dual nature of particles and all electromagnetic radiation, 'tendencies to exist' and 'tendencies to occur', the equivalence of force and matter, the interrelatedness of all phenomena and the universe as a dynamic web of energy patterns.

According to Hinduism and other Eastern philosophical traditions, the mystical experience of reality is a momentous event, which shatters the very foundations of one's view of the world based on sensory perceptions. Physicists are now in a similar situation since the concepts on which they based their scientific view of the world have been rudely shattered by the reality revealed by research into the sub-atomic world. The new view of reality that has emerged in physics however shows a close affinity with the philosophical ideas of the Eastern religious traditions. These similarities will be explored in the following chapters.

CHAPTER 2

THE ONENESS OF THE UNIVERSE

According to Advaita Vedanta, which embodies the essence of Hindu philosophy, the **sole reality is Existence-Consciousness.** It is a unity - an indivisible whole; unchanging, eternal and infinite. It has been referred to as Brahman or the Self; and **the world is an appearance of this reality. The world has its basis in Brahman.**

"Wherein stays all this universe; whereof all this is; wherefrom all this universe arises; wherefore is all this; whereby all this universe rises; which all this becomes - that alone is the Existence-Reality. That form let us place in our heart." (Ramana Maharshi - Invocation to the Supplement to the Forty Verses on Reality)

"The nature of reality is eternal existence; all pervasive existence; and existence underlying all forms, all transformations, all forces, all matter and all spirit. The Reality is the 'one' or unity behind the knower, the process of knowledge and the known. These are merely appearances, whereas the Reality lies beyond and behind them. They are like a mirage over the Reality - the result of delusion." (Talks Number 28)

"Appearance merely proves that something is, and no more. It would be wrong to think that what in it the senses seize exhausts its real being and substance." (Guru Vachaka Kovai Saying 637)

"The One only which exists is Reality. It is the Existence that appears as the world - the things we see and we ourselves. That which exists, exists for ever." (Talks Number 186)

"Reality is That which 'is'. Everything else is only an appearance and transient, but we confound the appearance with the Reality that is their substratum." (Talks Number 238)

"The Self is the ever-present Reality There is nothing else. As long as one identifies with a body, there appears to be a real world outside. But once the Self is realized, all these unrealities disappear leaving behind the knowledge that they are no other than the Self." (Talks Number 353)

"If, like the Lord, the world and I were real, His wholeness would be flawed. Unless we grant that the Lord could be divided, the world and 'I' can never claim reality." (Guru Vachaka Kovai Saying 112)

"Reality must always be real. It is not with forms and names but it is That which underlies them. It underlies limitations, being itself limitless. It underlies unrealities, being itself real. Reality is that which 'is'. It is as it is. It transcends language and expressions such as existence, non-existence etc." (Talks Number 140)

"Perception of a body and the world is because there is a 'body consciousness'. This springs from an 'I' consciousness, which in turn rises from Consciousness But in reality, Consciousness alone exists. All else are superimpositions thereon." (Talks Number 340)

"Brahman is pure spirit - formless, unlimited, eternal and without any differentiation. It is a unity. It never rises nor disappears. So it is permanent and therefore real - not transient and illusory." (Talks Number 363)

The Oneness of the Universe

"The Self is the only Reality - always there and eternally the same. It is simple 'Being', and since one cannot deny one's 'being', it is within everyone's experience This becomes clear only when one's tendency to objectify is overcome. It is the objectifying tendency that confounds the Self with the body - resulting in the false 'ego' (sense of individuality) and consequently the false world appearance". (Talks Number 46)

Brahman is said to be identical with the world in the sense that the world is not apart from Brahman. At the same time it is not identical with the world because Brahman, being real, cannot be subject to the changes in the world. One of the criteria of reality is immutability. Brahman therefore does not undergo a transformation in appearing as the world. The transformation is only an apparent one. The material cause (Brahman) brings about an effect (the world appearance) that is not different from the cause. **Brahman and the world are a unity and co-exist as reality and appearance.**

"The world is real and unreal at the same time in the sense that it is real as the Self and unreal apart from the Self. In the words of Sankara - Brahman is real; the world is unreal; Brahman is the world." (Talks Number 315)

"There is no being who is not conscious and therefore not Siva (Brahman). Not only is he Siva, but all else of which he is aware or not aware is also Siva. In ignorance he thinks he sees a world of diverse forms but if he 'sees' his self, he is not aware of any separateness from the world. The sense of his separateness and that of all else vanishes, although they persist in all their forms. Siva is seen as all i.e. as the substratum of all. Siva is the Being assuming these forms as well as the consciousness that sees them. But the ordinary person sees only the forms and not Siva (the reality) in these forms." (Talks Number 450)

"There is only one Consciousness which, manifesting as the 'I' thought and identifying itself with a body, projects itself

through the eyes and sees a world of objects outside. Being limited in the wakeful state, it expects to see something apart from itself and the evidence of the senses is the seal of authority. In this state, one will not admit that the seer, the seen and the seeing are all manifestations of the one Consciousness - the real 'I'. In truth there is nothing visual." (Talks Number 196)

"There is neither a seer nor the seen but only the Self. Nothing - seer nor seen - can exist apart from the Self just as no pictures can be seen without the screen." (Day by Day with Bhagavan; 17-10-46)

The world is not the essential truth but merely the phenomenal truth of Brahman. The finite world is, in truth, the infinite Brahman but this Infinite is hidden from our view. The cause of the appearance of the world and our taking it for real is in the nature of the human intellect and its cognitive mechanism which depends on the senses. **We rely on the sense and intellect and accept the pluralistic world as real, whereas the reality is the indivisible whole or Brahman.**

"The world is of the form of the five (types of) sense objects, and nothing else. Those five-fold sense objects are the spheres of the five sense organs. Since the one mind (intellect) understands the world through the channels of these sense organs, say, is there a world (plurality) other than the mind?" (Verse 6. Forty Verses on Reality)

Advaita Vedanta asserts that it is the intellect that fragments the world into separate objects and events. This fragmentation is not a fundamental feature of reality viz. Brahman, but merely an abstraction devised by our discriminating and categorizing intellect. The cause of the appearance of the world is therefore in the nature of the intellect and not in the nature of Brahman. **Brahman exists entire and undivided, and the appearance of plurality is due to the intellect that works in the logical mode of space, time and causality.** As we perceive through our senses, whereas the reality is beyond the senses, we accept the pluralistic universe for the reality of the unitary Brahman, of which it is an effect. The tendency to confuse the transcendental with the empirical is natural to the human mind. It is the result of our cognitive mechanism and the nature of our intellect. **To believe that our abstract concepts of separate 'things' and 'events' are realities of nature is therefore an illusion.**

The illusion that the perceived objects constituting the world appearance are real is attributed, in Advaita Vedanta, to 'avidya', which translates literally as false knowledge. It is therefore another name for ignorance. We cannot possibly reach true knowledge of the Reality so long as we are subject to the logical mode of thinking that is natural to the human mind.

'Avidya' is an innate obscuration of reality caused by a twist of mind that makes it impossible for us to see except through the texture of space-time-cause. It thereby shuts us off from our own reality and that of the world

The false knowledge or 'avidya' is dispelled, according to Advaita, by overcoming its cause viz. by transcending the intellect that creates the illusion of the reality of the world. One then realizes, by direct mystic experience, that Brahman is in the world, though not the world appearance. The world is seen to be illusory, but not in the sense of non-being Just as a mirage exists because there is a basis for its appearance, so does the world exist because it has a basis viz. Brahman. All phenomena or appearances are expressions of the infinite Brahman that is their ground i.e. the reality behind them.

"Unity is the Reality. The perceived variety of forms is false and obstructs knowledge of the unity of Reality." (Talks Number 354)

"Maya or illusion cannot obscure the Absolute Being but it does obscure absolute knowledge by making it appear

differentiated into particulars. Just as in dim light a rope appears as a snake, so does Absolute Being - the substratum - appear as the universe because of Maya." *(Talks Number 100)*

"To those who have not realized, as well as to those who have realized, the world is real. To those who have not realized, the reality is of the measure of the world. The reality, to those who have realized, is formless and shines as the ground of the world. This is the difference between the two." *(Verse 18. Forty Verses on Reality)*

"Both the 'jnani' and the 'ajnani' perceive the world but their outlooks differ. The former is aware of the real viz. the substratum of the world appearance, but the latter perceives only the superficial appearance." *(Talks Number 65)*

"Pure Being, the nature of our Self, That alone exists eternally. Apart from That, all objects that we see are clusters of illusive appearances that come and go while That, unmoving and unchanged, abides the same forever." *(Guru Vachaka Kovai Saying 980)*

"The 'jnani' sees only the Self and all in the Self. An analogy is the mirror and the reflections therein. To see the mirror (which alone is real) it is not necessary that one should cease to see the reflections therein (the world appearance)." *(Day by Day with Bhagavan; 6-3-46)*

"One must first realize that there is nothing but the Self and that he is that Self. Only then can he see everything as forms of that Self. One must therefore turn the mind inwards; see oneself as the Self within; and then see the Self that is within oneself in everything. In such 'seeing' there is no seer and seen. Self alone exists. It is both seer and seen and above seeing and being seen." *(Day by Day with Bhagavan; 18-4-46)*

The Oneness of the Universe

"He who sees the Self sees only the Self in the world It is immaterial whether the world appears or not. His attention is on the Self." (Day by Day with Bhagavan; 17-8-46)

"There seem to be as many 'I's as there are bodies. But, in truth, they are all one 'I' - the Self alone. Become yourself the one integral Being-Awareness and behold all 'I's together as one Self." (Guru Vachaka Kovai Saying 843)

"Just as on a cinema screen, there can be a scene in which a spectator watches events unfolding in a drama, so does an illusory being watch an illusory world in real life during the waking state." (Talks Number 443)

"In our true Self, which is supreme Being-Awareness, we conceive a little 'self' and so create a world of ignorance in which the supreme Self seems non-existent." (Guru Vachaka Kovai Saying 982)

"Mind is merely identification of the Self with the body. This identification creates the false 'ego' (the sense of individual being) and this, in turn, creates false phenomena (the illusory world appearance). The Self is the only reality. If the false identification vanishes, the eternal presence of the Self - the Reality - becomes apparent." (Talks Number 46)

"When the sense that 'I am the body' dies, all troublesome illusions and confusions vanish once for all. Within the heart explored, appears as 'I'-'I', the non-dual Self of pure Awareness." (Guru Vachaka Kovai Saying 866)

The above Advaitic philosophy regarding the world is based on mystical experience, which is a direct and non-intellectual experience of reality. The fundamental features of this philosophy are very similar to those now emerging from modern physics. Its essence is an awareness of the unity and inter-relation of all things and events; they are now seen as manifestations of a basic 'oneness' - the one ultimate 'Cosmic

Whole' that is the sole reality. **The basic oneness of the universe has been one of the most important revelations of modern physics - manifesting more and more as research has penetrated deeper and deeper into the nature of matter and reached the realm of sub-atomic particles.** *Here, the constituents of matter, and the phenomena involving them, have been found to be inter-connected and inter-dependent. They cannot be understood as isolated entities but only as parts integrated into the whole.*

To see and believe in the diversity, plurality and separateness of world phenomena is an illusion. In the mystic experience, all the diverse phenomena in the world are experienced as manifestations of a basic oneness. All things and events are inter-dependent and inseparable - being different forms or manifestations of the same ultimate reality, which is intrinsically indivisible. This great all-encompassing 'whole' is the oneness of the totality of all things.

According to Advaita Vedanta, the main aim of life in the world is therefore the transcending of this illusion, so that the basic unity of the universe or Brahman is directly experienced. When 'avidya'- the cause of the illusion - is overcome, the appearance of the world will vanish. The appearance will stand transfigured in the Absolute The false knowledge of plurality is removed by perfect knowledge There is therefore no plurality apart from the individual's 'avidya'. In perfect knowledge i.e. knowledge of the reality, the world is not so much negated as re-interpreted.

"When one loses one's moorings and leaves one's original state of Self, one identifies with a body and sees the world as separate from him. He should track back to his source, the Self, and abide therein. It will then be found, by direct experience, that there is nothing apart from the Self." (Talks. Number 252)

"Far from revealing the Truth, words only darken and conceal It. To let the Truth shine of itself, instead of burying it in

words, merge in the heart both word and thought." (Guru Vachaka Kovai Saying 525)

"Let not your intellect become a slave to the mere sound and fury of controversy. Enter the heart with mind pellucid, concept-free, and realize your natural Being as the Truth." (Guru Vachaka Kovai Saying 526)

"Relative knowledge pertains to the mind and not to the Self. It is therefore illusory and impermanent – appearing in the wakeful state and vanishing in sleep. One should go beyond such relative knowledge and abide in the Self. Such experience is real knowledge - not just what is apprehended by the mind." (Talks. Number 285)

"The false identification of the Self with the body is due to thoughts, which arise because of the 'I' thought (sense of individual existence). If this root thought is quelled, all other thoughts are quashed. The real Self will shine forth of itself and everything becomes known. Self-realization is thus our primary and sole duty." (Talks Number 379)

"The Self is alone pure knowledge. Relative knowledge is only conceptual whereas true or pure knowledge is direct experience. Experience is not possible without simultaneous knowledge of it. It is a far more subtle form of knowledge than even the subtlest relative knowledge." (Talks Number 204)

"However much one learns, there will be no bounds to (relative) knowledge. If on the other hand, one investigates the mind - the knower of relative knowledge - it is eliminated and the Self alone remains. This is the state of wisdom (freedom from thoughts), where oneself and the world are found to be the Self (God)." (Talks Number 238)

"If oneself be with form, the world and the Supreme will also be so (with form). But if one is without form, then who will see the

form of those, and how? Verily, oneself is the Eye, the Endless Eye." (Verse 4. Forty Verses on Reality.)

"Perception implies the existence of a seer and the seen. The seer is intimate - being our Self - whereas the seen is alien to the seer. We do not however turn our attention to knowing the self-evident seer but expend effort on analyzing the seen. The more the mind is expanded in this way, the farther it goes away from the Self. We must directly see the seer and thus realize the Self." (Talks Number 427)

"Knowledge does not consist in knowing objects. This is relative knowledge. Pure knowledge or absolute knowledge stands all alone - the One, Unique Transcendent Light of Pure Consciousness. We are not independent of this Pure Knowledge because IT alone exists. Ignorance comprising thought interposing, Pure Knowledge seems different from what it really is. It is seen as 'I' and the world." (Talks Number 589)

"Leaving out the seeing Self which is most intimate and immediate, we seek the rest i.e. get involved in studies of the world. We cannot therefore realize that our Self is also the Self immanent in the world." (Talks Number 639)

"What is worth seeking and discovering is the truth of Self. Such knowledge comes only to the still, clear intellect not muddled by strenuous search without, but questing within for the Truth in silence." (Guru Vachaka Kovai Saying 433)

"Since Being is one and never dual, true knowing is not knowing something else. It is but the clarity, the tranquil peace of the mind when undeluded by the senses and so standing still." (Guru Vachaka Kovai Saying 437)

"The differences in the world appearance are superficial. A Unity runs through the diversity. It is the Self (Brahman). Perception of this unity is true knowledge and joy that dispels

The Oneness of the Universe

all the sorrows that arise from taking the diversity for real."
(Talks Number 507)

"After the experience of the 'samadhi' or mystic state, the world will be taken only at its true worth i.e. merely as a manifestation of the Reality. World phenomena, being known to be illusory, will leave one unaffected." (Talks Number 465)

"As long as there is a subject 'I', thoughts will arise and objects will appear. If the subject is sought and known, the objects merge in the subject. Without that knowledge, one applies the mind to objects which appear to exist on their own and does not know that one's true nature is the Self that is the substratum and sole Reality behind both subject and objects."
(Talks Number 634)

"The sense perceptions that persuade us that the phenomenal world is real pervert the truth. The senses that perceive and the perceiver are, like the phenomena they perceive, mere appearance, no more." (Guru Vachaka Kovai Saying 871)

Quantum theory has revealed the essential interconnectedness of the universe. It cannot be decomposed into independently existing smaller units. Isolated material particles have been shown to be mere abstractions – their properties being definable and observable only through their interaction with other systems. They are thus merely idealizations with no fundamental significance.

At the atomic level, the solid material objects of classical physics have been found to dissolve into patterns of probabilities; and these probabilities are not of things but of interconnections. The universe is seen, not as a collection of physical objects, but as a complex web of relations between parts of a unified whole.

"The world appears as a complicated tissue of events in which connections of various kinds alternate and overlap and thereby determine the texture of the whole." [1]

"There cannot be things as separate parts and separate events in the universe since it is a unified whole that cannot yield to division." [2]

The fundamental features of the Vedic philosophy based on direct mystic experience have thus begun to emerge in modern physics. Its essence is an awareness of the unity and inter-relation of all things and events, since they are now seen as manifestations of a basic oneness - the one, ultimate cosmic 'whole' that is the sole reality. This concept of the universe as an indivisible and integrated whole has been carried even further in the so-called 'bootstrap theory' of modern physics. This theory is dealt with more fully in a later chapter. Briefly, it states that every particle consists of all other particles in the sense that they are not separate entities; they are inter-related energy patterns involved in organized dynamic processes with one another. The universe is a dynamic web of inter-related events. None of the properties of any part of this web is fundamental. They all flow from the properties of the web. The overall consistency of their inter-relations determines the entire web. Unity is thus based on inter-relations.

"The unity of the cosmos is now supported by developments in cosmology too. They suggest that everyday conditions could not present themselves here but for the distant parts of the universe. Our ideas of space and geometry would be invalid if these parts were taken away." [3]

Such expressions of the unity of the universe were expressed in Vedic philosophy thousands of years ago. Swami Vivekananda expressed it forcefully when he declared:

"One atom of the universe cannot move without dragging the whole universe with it." [4]

The Oneness of the Universe

This notion of unbroken wholeness denies the classical idea that the universe can be divided into separate and independently existing parts. *Classical physics postulated that independent elementary parts were the fundamental reality, and the various systems were merely particular contingent forms and arrangements of these parts. Quantum theory has however now shown that the inseparable quantum interconnectedness of the universe is the fundamental reality, while the parts are merely particular contingent forms within the closely integrated whole.*

The picture of an 'unbroken wholeness', being the reality underlying the universe is also one of the fundamental features of the mystic experience in Hinduism. This indivisible wholeness - the essence and substratum of the universe - is known in Advaita Vedanta as Brahman. Maharshi however referred to it most commonly as the Self. The term emphasizes the nature of Reality as being the true 'I', which is a non-personal, all-inclusive awareness and not an experience of individuality. He also equated Brahman or the Self with God as the universe is sustained by the power of the Self, and theists normally attribute this power to God. **Maharshi's God is therefore not a personal God but the immanent formless Being that sustains the universe.**

"God is none other than Absolute Being or the Self. Knowing the Self, God is known. Since nothing is more intimate knowledge than our sense of being i.e. the ego or 'I' thought, this should be the starting point to know God - not anything external that is not directly known. Such enquiry leads to the Self (God), as it is the source of the ego." (Talks 106)

"The Lord supreme, as flawless true Awareness, stands for ever – whole and sole – not to be known as This or That, even for worship. For one to claim separate being apart from him is sheer ignorance." (Guru Vachaka Kovai Saying 776)

"God is 'all that is' plus the Being; the ego 'I' is individuality plus the Being; and the world is all the perceived diversity plus the Being. In all cases, the Being is alone real, while the 'all that is', the individuality and the diversity are unreal adjuncts. Reality is pure being (without any adjuncts)." *(Talks Number 112)*

"The gods we earnestly worship appear and disappear by turns. The natural Awareness that abides ever unchanging, clear and certain is the real god supreme." *(Guru Vachaka Kovai saying 1073)*

"Images of God are merely symbols of That which lies beyond all forms - the Reality. One is really formless, but so long as one believes that one has a physical form, worship of God with a form is not inappropriate." *(Talks Numbers 133, 121)*

"Abiding thought-free as the mere I AM, it is best to worship formless Being pure. But till one is qualified for such worship of the Formless Absolute, 'tis meet to worship God with form." *(Guru Vachaka Kovai Saying 658)*

"You who do not feel the secret melting power of image worship and so condemn it, why then do you cherish this flawed crawling body, mistaking it for you." *(Guru Vachaka Kovai Saying 208)*

"So long as there is duality, there will be God and devotee. Realizing the God of devotion (through surrender) there will be unity only - just as upon merging into the Source through the path of enquiry, there is Unity." *(Talks Number 154)*

"There is no 'all' apart from God for him to pervade. He alone 'is'." *(Talks Number 268)*

The Unity of the Observer and the Observed

In Eastern mysticism, the universal interwoven-ness always includes the person and his consciousness. *Atomic physics too has revealed the fact that the interwoven-ness of the universe actually includes the observer and his consciousness. 'Objects' can only be understood in terms of a chain of interaction between the processes of preparation and measurement; and this chain of processes ends in the consciousness of the observer Measurements are really interactions that create 'sensations' in the consciousness of the observer if he lets them interact with him.*

Another crucial and related fact that has emerged from atomic physics is that the observer is necessary not only to observe the properties of an 'object' but also to define these properties. This is because these properties have meaning only in the context of the interaction of the 'object' with the observer. So *what one observes in experiments is not nature itself, but nature as exposed to our method of questioning. If the experimental arrangements are altered, the properties of the observed object will be different!*

In atomic physics therefore, the scientist cannot be a detached objective observer. He is involved in the world he observes to the extent that he influences the properties of what is being observed. *The concept of a world as 'sitting out there' and apart from the observer is thus destroyed.* To make his observations, the atomic physicist has to reach in to install his measuring equipment; the type of equipment that he installs limits the nature of the measurement; and the measurement itself changes the state of the object being measured. Really, it is therefore a case of participation rather than observation. In some strange sense, the universe is a participatory universe. Relativity theory thus suggests that consciousness is the 'basic stuff' of the universe since the observer is not outside the phenomenon he studies. Both are bound together in the same consciousness. The observer is a participant in a Reality that is Consciousness.

"The knower and the known are therefore just two different aspects of the one Cosmic Consciousness." [5]

"The observing mind and the observed are inter-related in a real and fundamental sense." [6]

In the Vedic mystic experience too, mystical knowledge of the reality behind the universe is never obtained by objective observation, but involves full participation with one's whole being. In the mystic experience, the observer and the observed are not only inseparable but actually become indistinguishable. In the state of enlightenment, the distinction between observer and observed breaks down completely, and the observer (subject) and observed (object) fuse into one undifferentiated whole. **The final realization of the unity of all things is reached, according to the mystics, in a state where one's individual consciousness dissolves into an infinite undifferentiated consciousness.** Here the world of the senses is transcended; duality ceases; and the notion of 'things' is finally abandoned.

"How can the ego 'I' imagine itself as That, when That – its source – can only be attained after destroying utterly this 'I'? The right way is, the ego gone, abiding in the Heart in silence." (Guru Vachaka Kovai Saying 740)

"The mind (individual consciousness) turned outwards results in thoughts and the world (of diversity). Turned inwards it becomes the Self." (Day by Day with Bhagavan; 8-1-45)

"When the source of the ego 'I' is traced, it is seen to have no separate existence. It merges in the real 'I'." (Day by Day with Bhagavan; 2-1-46)

"First one sees the Self as the world; then as a 'void'; and finally as Self. But in the last, there is no objective seeing. Here, seeing is being the Self. The progression results from giving up (objective) awareness of what is non-self, until finally only pure awareness remains." (Day by Day with Bhagavan; 21-7-46)

"Inward in the heart enquiring keenly 'Who am I?' - the seeker vanishes and Siva alone shines clear. When the avid beholder does not exist, it would be madness to say that the world beheld exists." (Guru Vachaka Kovai Saying 110)

"The 'sattvic' or pure mind is the Absolute Consciousness. What is witnessed (the observed) and the witness (the observer) merge in this state, in which Absolute Consciousness reigns supreme. It is not a state of 'sunya' (blank). It is the real Self." (Talks. Number 68)

"When relative consciousness vanishes in meditation, it is realization and not annihilation of the Self because Absolute Consciousness arises in place of limited consciousness. With Absolute Consciousness realized, if one looks outwards, the universe is seen to be not apart from the realized Absolute Consciousness." (Talks. Number 311)

"When the projector's light is lost in broad daylight, the pictures vanish. Even so, when the mind's borrowed light is lost in pure Awareness, the false grand show of jiva, God and world disappears." (Guru Vachaka Kovai Saying 114)

According to the concept of 'triputi' in Advaita Vedanta, the mind creates the trinity of observer, observation and observed by fragmenting and objectifying an indivisible whole viz. the Pure Consciousness or Self that is the reality pervading the universe. As there is no appearance of a universe in the absence of the mind, it is said to participate in the creation of the universe. This concept of a participatory universe has recently received support from modern physics, following studies of the sub-atomic world The 'participation' principle in physics, as enunciated by one of the greatest physicists of our times, closely reflects the concept of a participatory universe in Advaita Vedanta.

"Our perceiving self is nowhere to be found within the world picture because it is itself the picture. It is identical with the whole and therefore cannot be contained within it as a part." [7]

"If seer and object differed in being, seeing would be impossible. As seeing does occur, we needs must know that they are one in Being." (Guru Vachaka Kovai Saying 639)

Maharshi repeatedly emphasized the role of the mind or ego in creating the illusion that there is a real and independently existing world outside us.

"Thought activity is associated with rise of the ego - limited individual consciousness - in the dream and waking states, and it causes the perception and inference of a world sitting outside. The 'reality' of the world is created by the ego when it emerges and disappears when it subsides - like a spider producing and withdrawing its web." (Talks. Number 25)

"The world is not external. Impressions (of a world) cannot have an outside origin because the world can only be cognized by consciousness. The world does not assert its existence; it is merely our intermittent impression - disappearing, along with the ego, in the state of sleep and re-appearing, with the ego, in the wakeful state." (Talks. Number 53)

"Know that these countless things are pictures in a dream and none is real apart from the beholder. Shun this phantom world of names and forms and dwell in the pure, blissful being of Awareness." (Guru Vachaka Kovai Saying 293)

"Only so long as there is a 'knower' is there knowledge of all kinds – direct, inferential, intellectual etc. Should the knower

vanish, they all vanish with him. Their validity is of the same degree as his." (Talks. Number 93)

"If you refrain from looking at this or that or any other object, then by that overpowering look into absolute being, you become yourself the boundless space of pure Awareness, which alone is Real Being." (Guru Vachaka Kovai Saying 647)

"The Truth or Reality is the Self (Brahman). Everything that is perceived requires the Self as the perceiver and their reality is only of the same degree as that of the perceiver. They cannot exist without the perceiver (Self) and therefore they are not different from the Self. Subjects and objects all merge in the Self. In the Self or Reality, there is no seer or seen, as the seer and seen are the Self." (Talks. Number 145)

"The Self is ever present. The universe (only) appears after the emergence of the mind. The mind and the entire universe are all contained in the Self (Brahman) and cannot exist apart from the Self." (Talks. Number 293)

"It is a false belief that we are part of a world that exists apart from us. In reality, the world is within us, in our minds, since we see it only in the waking state when the mind has arisen. Since we exist always, even in sleep, we should be aware of the world in sleep also, if it existed apart from us. The Self is always aware. When the Self identifies with the ego (seer) there is a world (the seen). The creation of a subject-object relationship is the creation of the world. Both are creations in Pure Consciousness – the Self. If the subject-object relationship is eliminated, the Self alone remains. This relationship arises as a consequence of the rise of the 'I'-thought." (Talks. Number 453)

"Vedanta says that the cosmos springs into view simultaneously with the seer. There is no detailed process of creation. Theories of creation are for those who desire explanations for the existence of the world i.e. objective knowledge". (Talks. Number 651)

"What is seen is not external but internal because, if external, they must assert themselves without there being a seer. The basis for the existence of what is seen is only the seer." (Talks. Number 305)

"The world is not external. It is because you wrongly identify your Self with the body that you perceive a pluralistic world outside and its sufferings. But they are not real. If you seek and abide as the Reality, all these unreal perceptions will disappear. Therefore look within and see the Self. When you see your self as the Self, not as the body, then the world also appears as the Self (Brahman)." (Talks. Number 272)

"Only so long as there is a measurer, do measuring and things measured seem to be. But when the measurer 'sees' the Self, - true Being - and gets lost in It, all other things perish along with him and disappear." (Guru Vachaka Kovai Saying 528)

In the framework that it operates in, atomic physics cannot go that far in experiencing the unity of the universe. But it has come very close to the world-view revealed by Hindu mysticism. It has destroyed the concepts of fundamentally separate objects and accepted the concept of participator to replace that of observer of the universe. The most recent discoveries are now leading it to include human consciousness in its conception of the universe.

The Unity of Opposites

The unity of the universe implies that opposites are illusory. Eastern mystics have long asserted that opposites or contrasts are mere concepts created by thought, and are therefore relative. In the mystic experience where thought and intellectual concepts are transcended, all things and events are realized to

The Oneness of the Universe

be manifestations of a basic oneness. Mystics become aware that all opposites and contrasts are relative and bear a polar relationship within an all-embracing unity. The unity of opposites is experienced as a dynamic balance or interplay between the two extremes. The unity underlying the opposites is the truth or Reality, and it brings about the interplay. Attainment of such awareness that all opposites are polar and thus a unity is regarded as one of the highest aims of spiritual effort. It is the absolute point of view or the reality.

"Be in the Truth Eternal, beyond all earthly opposites." (The Bhagavad Gita)

"The dyads (opposites) and triads (perceptions) always subsist on the basis of the One. If one sees in one's heart as to what that One is, those (opposites and perceptions) will disappear. They that see (thus) are the seers of the truth. They are not perturbed. Thus should you see." (Verse 9. Forty Verses on Reality.)

"The Self alone is real. But because it is infinite i.e. all-inclusive, it does not give room for questions involving duality, such as its reality (existence) or its non-reality (non-existence). Therefore it is said to be neither real (existent) nor unreal (non-existent). Similarly, even though it is Consciousness, there is nothing for it to know or make itself known to, so it is described as neither sentient nor non-insentient. All the opposites of our sensory world are transcended in the Reality." (Spiritual Instruction. Chapter 3. 10)

"There is no duality. Our present knowledge (that opposites and duality are real) is due to the ego (individual consciousness) and the consequent creation of a subject-object relationship. Such (dualistic) knowledge is only relative to the knowing subject (the ego). The pure awareness that is the true nature of the Self is absolute knowledge. One should go beyond relative knowledge and abide in the Self." (Talks. Number 285)

"The universe is now seen to be diverse but there is a common factor underlying all this diversity. So there is a unity behind the diversity. Opposites are only apparent and not real." (Talks. Number 319)

The concept of a dynamic unity of polar opposites is illustrated by the analogy of the circular motion of a billiard ball projected on a flat screen. The actual circular motion of the ball appears on the flat screen as an oscillation between two opposite points, but in the movement itself, the opposites are unified and transcended.

Modern physics has also now reached a stage where exploration of the sub-atomic world has revealed a reality where seemingly opposite and contradictory concepts are unified. A 'higher plane' similar to the higher plane of consciousness of Eastern mysticism - where thought and language are transcended and all opposites appear as a dynamic unity - has been reached. Examples of such unification of opposite concepts are the destructible and indestructible nature of matter, its discontinuous and continuous nature as particles and waves, rest and motion, and the revelation that force and matter are but different aspects of the same phenomenon. These traditional concepts are transcended by going to a higher dimension viz. that of four-dimensional space-time.

Seemingly opposite entities become unified in a higher dimension. In the analogy of the circular motion of a ball and its projection on a flat screen, the opposite poles of the oscillation in one dimension (along a line) are unified in the circular motion in two dimensions (in one plane). *The unification of entities that seem irreconcilable and separate is achieved in relativity theory by going from three to four dimensions. The four dimensional world of relativistic physics is the world where force and matter are unified; and where matter can appear as separate particles or as a continuous field.*

Modern physics has shown that the relativistic space-time reality is an intrinsically dynamic reality, where objects are also processes and forms are not static shapes but dynamic patterns. *This reality is however experienced in physics only through abstract mathematical formulations since visual imagination and ordinary language are limited to the 3-dimensional world of the senses – not to the multidimensional reality of relativistic physics.*

Eastern mystics have, on the other hand, been able to experience the higher dimensional reality directly and concretely. In the state of consciousness called 'samadhi' - also called the state of Self realization - they transcend the 3-dimensional world of everyday life and experience a totally different reality where all opposites are unified into an organic whole. This mystical experience cannot be described on the plane of 3-dimensional consciousness.

"Real waking lies beyond the plane of differences. All the perceived differences are thoughts. It is thought that obscures the Reality Real waking is awareness of the Reality, which is beyond the three states (of waking, dream and sleep)." (Talks. Number 476)

"In the state of 'samadhi' (the state of awareness of reality) there is Being alone. There is no I, nor you nor he; no present, nor past nor future. It is beyond time and space; beyond expression. Being is ever there, underlying the states of waking, dream and sleep as the reality." (Talks Number 17)

"Realization is Perfection. It cannot be comprehended by the mind. One must transcend the mind to be the Self, which is absolute knowledge. The present knowledge - of the mind - is only of limitation The absolute knowledge (of the Self) is unlimited. Being so, it cannot be comprehended by relative knowledge. Cease to be a knower. Then there is perfection." (Talks Number 147)

"Realization implies perfection. When one is limited (in the waking state), perception is also limited and so one's knowledge is imperfect. Of what use is imperfect knowledge? Perfect knowledge can only be in Self realization." (Talks Number 437)

"The state of realization is often called 'jagrat sushupti' i.e. wakeful sleep or sleeping wakefulness. There is the awareness of the waking state and the stillness of sleep. It is the state of perfect awareness and perfect stillness combined. It is the source from which thoughts spring and make all the difference between the stillness of sleep and the turmoil of waking. In Self realization, the stillness is reached with perfect awareness." (Talks Number 609)

The fundamental unity of space and time is the basis for the unification of all other opposite concepts. The opposites are a dynamic unity because relativistic space-time is an intrinsically dynamic reality.

The best instance of unification of contradictory concepts – apart from the relativity theory that unifies force and matter – is the unification of the concepts of particles and waves in atomic physics. At the atomic level, matter has been shown to have a dual aspect. It can appear as particles or as waves. The statement that the particle is also a wave means that the wave pattern as a whole is a manifestation of the particle. All forms of electromagnetic radiation, which includes light, also exhibit this dual nature. Light is emitted and absorbed in the form of 'quanta' or photons, but when these particles of light travel through space, they appear as vibrating electric and magnetic fields that behave just like waves. Electrons also behave like waves when they exhibit diffraction just like light.

Existence and non-existence constitute another pair of opposites that is transcended by atomic reality. In the sub-atomic world, it is not possible to say definitely that an atomic particle exists at a particular place or that it does not exist there. Being a probability pattern, the particle merely has tendencies to exist in various places, and thus manifests a strange kind of physical reality between existence and non-existence. The state of a particle is indescribable in terms of the concept of fixed opposites. The particle is not present in a definite place but neither is it absent. It does not change its position, nor is it at rest. What changes is the probability pattern, and thus the tendencies to exist in certain places.

This strange kind of reality between existence and non-existence also applies to the Reality or Brahman experienced by the Hindu mystic. Brahman lies beyond existence and non-existence and is the basis of the world. The relation of being i.e. existence, to non-being i.e. non-existence, in the finite world is regarded, not as one of exclusion but one of polar opposition. The two are, at the same time, antithetical and correlative. Neither of them attains actuality except through its contrast with the other.

Modern physics has thus confirmed one of the basic postulates of Eastern mysticism viz. that all the concepts we use to describe and understand nature are limited. It has shown that they are not features of reality, but mere creations of the human mind. Whenever we expand the realm of our experience beyond that of the senses, the limitations of our rational mind become apparent and we have to modify or even abandon many of these concepts. Both modern physics and Eastern mysticism are sciences concerned with such experience involving phenomena beyond the realm of sensory experience, and it is therefore not surprising that they have arrived at the same conclusion viz. that our perceptions of reality are merely conceptual and not the true nature of reality.

"The world, (the sense of) individuality and God (as a person) are all conceptions of the false 'I'. If they were real, they should appear in sleep also, since one does not cease to exist in

sleep. They are all dependent upon the false 'I' or 'I'-thought." (Talks. Number 197)

"Please do not debate, good folk, whether heaven and hell exist. As long, as much, as this - our world - exists, so long, so much they too exist." (Guru Vachaka Kovai Saying 178)

"Brahman - also called the Heart - is the sole reality. It is the Source from which all thoughts arise and on which they subsist. These thoughts are the content of our mind and shape the universe (that we perceive)." (Talks Number 97)

"The perceived existence and awareness of the physical world are simultaneous and coincide with rise of the mind. So both are part of the existence of the mind and its awareness. The substratum of the mind is the Self (Brahman), which is self-existent and eternally aware." (Talks. Number 381)

"As in the sky with thick clouds covered, no eye can see the glorious sun, so does one fail to see one's own Self when the mind firmament is darkened by a dense cloud of thoughts." (Guru Vachaka Kovai Saying 917)

"It is possible to accept the world as imagination or the product of thought if the mind, which comprehends the physical space, is itself conceived as space. The mind ether is contained in transcendental ether (Consciousness) and itself contains physical ether Thoughts arising in transcendental ether and appearing in mind ether result in physical objects in physical ether - thus creating the world appearance." (Talks. Number 451)

"Knowledge of objects is based on one's awareness of them. Their existence is not absolute because one cannot postulate their existence in the absence of one's awareness of them." (Talks. Number 507)

"The world appears distinctly only in wakefulness and dream, with concepts filled. In concept-free, all empty sleep, one sees no world. So then conceptual is the world's whole substance." (Guru Vachaka Kovai Saying 29)

"There is nothing but the Atman. The mind originates from the Atman and projects the world." (Talks. Number 104)

"When the mind, through the brain and senses, outward turns, the names and forms are from within thrust out. And when the mind at rest abides within the Heart, they enter and lie buried there again." (Guru Vachaka Saying 32)

"Mind is only a multitude of thoughts that arise because there is a thinker. The ego is the thinker i.e. the root thought from which all other thoughts arise. If the ego is sought, it vanishes automatically. It follows that all other thoughts such as of a world; birth and death; pain and pleasure will disappear too." (Talks Number 195)

"If, by the practice of self-enquiry, the ego dies, nothing henceforth is seen as alien. What was falsely known before as objects, is experienced now as the very Self of which Advaita speaks." (Guru Vachaka Kovai saying 767)

"The absolute truth is the 'ajata doctrine' which says that nothing exists except the one unity. To such as find it difficult to grasp this truth, - being unable to ignore the solid world they see around them - the 'drishti-shristi' doctrine is given. This says that, as in the dream experience, all that one sees depends on the seer. Apart from the seer, there is no seen. One first creates out of one's mind (through thought) and then sees (and takes for real) what one's mind itself has created." (Day by Day with Bhagavan; p 149)

"The world is not perceived in your sleep although you cannot deny your existence in that state. The world appears when you wake up. Clearly, the world is your thought. Thoughts are

your projections. The 'I' is first created and then the world. The world is created by the 'I' that - in its turn - rises up from the Self." (Talks. Number 455)

"Seen in the light of Self-experience, all this phenomenal world is mere appearance – like the sky's deep blueness. What the deluded, body-bound ego perceives 'out there' is mind created, - nothing more." (Guru Vachaka Kovai Saying 39)

"Although the world and our awareness of the world rise and set as one, it is by the awareness that the world shines. The Whole, wherefrom the world and its awareness rise and wherein they set, but which shines without rising or setting, That alone is real." (Verse 7. Forty Verses on Reality)

CHAPTER 3

THE UNREALITY OF SPACE AND TIME

Classical physics was based on two fundamental notions. One was that of an absolute three-dimensional space that was independent of the material objects it contained and which obeyed the laws of Euclidean geometry. The other was that of time as a separate dimension from space and which was also absolute, and therefore flowed at an even rate independent of the material world.

Eastern religious traditions had however always maintained that space and time were constructs of the mind. They were therefore treated like all other intellectual concepts, - as being relative, limited and illusory. According to the mystics, notions of space and time were linked to a particular state of consciousness. Going beyond this ordinary state of consciousness, they had realized that the conventional notions of space and time were not the absolute truth.

According to the Eastern mystics, space and time are not the objective realities that we imagine they are, but creations of the ego or our sense of independent, separate existence. They are subjective mental forms that come into existence after the ego sense. Thus, in deep sleep there is neither space nor time; but when we awake, the ego rises saying 'I am the body' and, in so doing, creates space and time. The body and the world are located therein. When the ego disappears in the sleep state, these also disappear. *Time and space therefore have no existence apart from the ego.* Our experience that we are bound in space and time is merely an illusion caused by the notion 'I am the body'. The body alone is in time and space. The mystics, speaking from direct experience, assert that *we are, in reality, the pure, infinite and eternal consciousness that we always experience as 'I am'. This is our true self, but by confounding it with the body we give rise to the ego sense.*

Time and place appear in, and by, the real Self, which is pure Existence-Awareness, but is not affected by them. The real Self is timeless and spaceless. **Since time and space do not survive the disappearance of the ego, they are unreal since the absolute standard of reality includes the criteria of changelessness and continuity of existence.**

Since time does not really exist for the real Self, the absolute truth is that there is no past nor future - or even the present (in the sense that this concept is normally understood). All events that assume the reality of time are also unreal. Therefore we have had no past births, nor shall we have any future births; we are even now not embodied, so death is unreal. Neither can there be actions done in the past, whose consequences must be experienced in the future. Similarly, since space is also an illusion, the distinction between inside and outside is also unreal and so the world appearance - which depends on this distinction - cannot be an objective reality. If there is no outside, there cannot be a multitude of inanimate objects or a multiplicity of living beings in an outside space.

The above statement is the absolute, unadulterated truth regarding Reality as experienced by all sages, and was always expressed in unequivocal terms by Ramana Maharshi to persons who were ready to receive this teaching. Such readiness is the intellectual conviction that our real self is not the ego but something beyond and from which it rises. This however does not affect the validity of the beliefs of the ordinary person so long as he lives in the world or relativity - by confounding his true Self with the illusory ego.

"On enquiry, where is time and where is space, apart from us? If we are the bodies, we shall be involved in time and space.

The Unreality of Space and Time

(But) are we the bodies? We are the same, now, then, and ever. We are the same here, there and everywhere. Know this: We are; time and space are not. We are." (Verse 16. Forty Verses on Reality)

"Time is only a concept. There is only the Reality. In the state of awareness of the Reality, there is 'Being' alone. There is no I, nor you, nor he. There is no present, nor past nor future. It is beyond time and space - beyond expression. 'Being' is ever there, underlying the states of waking, dream and sleep as the Reality." (Talks. Number 17)

"Time and space are only concepts of the human mind. The real Self (Brahman) is beyond mind, time and space." (Talks. Number 68)

"Without consciousness, time and space do not exist. Time and space appear in consciousness, which is like a lighted screen on which these are cast like pictures." (Talks. Number 199)

"Time and space operate on the plane of physical existence where one identifies with a body and is subject to limitations. The physical body is in space and time but in reality space and time are in you - the true Self." (Talks Number 304)

"We cannot deny our existence in the state of deep sleep, but in that state there is no perception of space and time - to be remembered upon waking. Since we are the same self throughout sleep and waking, it follows that there was no space or time in sleep to be remembered (upon waking). The space and time of the waking state are merely mental concepts that arise following the rise of the 'I'-thought (and mind) upon waking. The real 'I' - the Self - is unlimited, universal, and beyond time and space." (Talks. Number 311)

"If one recognizes the Self even in temporal phenomena (the world events that take place in time), these will be found to be

non-existent, i.e. not separate from the Self; and going on at the same time." (Talks Number 376)

"Questions about the future or the world will not arise for one who has reached the state beyond thought, because time and space are merely thoughts. In reality, there is no world or future. At this level, one is Infinite Intelligence - the Self. It is Perfection." (Talks Number 480)

"Time is the interval between two states and a state cannot come into being unless the mind calls it into existence. Therefore, if the mind is not functioning, there can be no concept of time. Time and space are in the mind, but one's true state is beyond the mind. The question of time does not arise for one established in his true state." (Talks. Number 601)

"Those who abide in their true Being know nothing but the Self, no time Much less do they perceive three tenses, separate parts in seamless time." (Guru Vachaka Kovai Saying 748)

The mystical experience of space and time is in many ways very similar to the view that has emerged in modern physics, as expressed in the theory of relativity. This new view of space and time says that all measurements of space and time are relative. It had long been recognized that spatial specifications such as left and right, or above and below, depend on the position of the observer The temporal order of events was however considered to be independent of any observer. It was Einstein who demonstrated that even temporal specifications are relative and depend on the observer. Time can be regarded as absolute only where – due to the near infinite velocity of light – we can correctly assume that we observe events at the instant of their occurrence. This applies to the world of our everyday experience. But in the sub-atomic world, where events are interactions between particles moving at velocities similar in magnitude to that of light, there can be a distinct lapse of time between the occurrence of an event and its observation. Different observers can perceive the same events as occurring in different temporal sequences depending on their respective positions and velocities relative to the events observed. The 'same' instant can thus differ from observer to observer. Also, there is no one moment that is 'now' for all observers.

As a result of the Special Theory of Relativity, concepts of space, time and motion have undergone a complete change. **Distance, time interval, speed and direction are all now regarded as relative concepts rather than absolute.** They are absolute only with reference to the world that we experience with our senses, since space, time and motion are merely constructs of the human mind. They have no reality when one transcends the mind and experiences the Absolute Reality that underlies the world of sensory experience. In the new relativistic framework, space and time are treated on an equal footing and are connected inseparably. Time is incorporated with the three space co-ordinates as a fourth co-ordinate that is specified relative to the observer Time is thus added to the three space dimensions as a fourth dimension. *Beyond the 'relative plane' of our usual waking consciousness, space and time form a four-dimensional space-time continuum. The whole universe is, in reality, one single unbroken continuum, so much so that one cannot talk about space without talking about time and vice versa when phenomena involving velocities of the order of that of light are described. The true account of an event can therefore be given by an observer only if it is viewed in four dimensional space-time.*

Einstein's theory of relativity has thus led to abandonment of the idea that space and time are separate and absolute, and that they have any objective significance as separate physical entities. Distance, time interval, speed and direction are now regarded as relative concepts rather than absolute. They are absolute only with reference to the world we experience with our senses, since space, time and motion are merely constructs of the human mind. They have no reality when one transcends the mind and experiences the absolute Reality that underlies the world of sensory experience. *Relativity theory thus implies that space and time are only elements of a language used by observers to understand and interpret particular situations or events in their sensory environment.* Such a view closely parallels the view held by the mystics, who have always held that space and time are nothing but forms of thought or words of common usage.

As indicated earlier, this unification of space and time entailed a unification of other basic concepts and this unifying aspect is the most important feature of the relativistic framework. Concepts that seemed totally in opposition are now seen to be merely different aspects of one and the same concept.

All these relativistic effects seem strange and paradoxical to us because we cannot experience the 4-dimensional space-time world or the other relativistic concepts through our senses. They can experience only the 3-dimensional images of the 4-dimensional world of reality. These images appear different in different frames of reference. They are only illusory projections of 4-dimensional phenomena, just as shadows are 2-dimensional projections of 3- dimensional objects, and oscillation between two extreme points is the illusory projection on a flat screen of the real circular motion of a body. If one could visualize the 4-dimensional reality, there would be no paradoxes at all.

According to Hinduism, mystics attain a non-ordinary state of consciousness in which they transcend the 3-dimensional world of everyday life to directly experience the higher multi-dimensional reality. The dimensions of these states may not be the same as the dimensions dealt with in relativistic physics, but it is striking that they have led mystics towards notions of space and time which are very similar to those implied by relativity theory. This non-ordinary state of consciousness is referred to as 'sahaja samadhi', in which one experiences a state of complete dissolution where there are no distinctions whatsoever. Everything is related to every other, not only spatially but also temporally. In this state, it is a fact of experience that there is no space without time; and no time without space.

"One experiences a state of complete dissolution where there is no more distinction between mind and body, subject and object. One looks around and perceives that every object is related to every other, not only spatially but also temporally. As a fact of pure experience, there is no space without time; no time without space. They are interpenetrating." [8]

"Mystics seem able to attain non-ordinary states of consciousness in which they transcend the three dimensional world of everyday life to experience a higher multi-dimensional reality of one infinite expanse of space and time." [9]

Because of the awareness that space and time are intimately connected and inter-penetrating, the worldviews of modern physics and Hindu mysticism are both intrinsically dynamic and contain time and change as essential elements. This similar awareness of the modern physicist and the mystic are both based on experience. In the case of the physicist, however, it is based on scientific experiments while in the case of the mystic, it is based upon mystical experience of a higher state of consciousness.

In the 'general theory of relativity', Einstein extended the framework of his 'special theory of relativity' - the basic features of which are the relativity of space and time and their unification into 4-dimensional 'space-time' – to include gravity The effect of gravity, according to the new theory, is to make space curved. This again is very difficult for us to imagine, since we cannot look at 3-dimensional space from the outside i.e. from 4-dimensional space. *However as Einstein proved, the 3-dimensional space in which we live is actually curved.* The curvature of space is caused by the gravitational field of massive bodies, and the degree of curvature depends on the mass of the massive body.

Since space cannot be separated from time in relativity theory, the curvature of space caused by gravity extends into 4-dimensional 'space-time' also. In curved 'space-time', the distortions caused by the curvature result in time not flowing universally at the same rate. *As the curvature varies from place to place, - according to the distribution of massive bodies – so does the flow of time.*

The 'general theory of relativity' therefore asserts not only that space and time are not absolute and independent entities and that all measurements of space and time are relative, but also that *the whole structure of 'space-time' is inextricably linked to the distribution of matter.* Space is curved to different degrees and time flows at different rates in different parts of the universe. Our notions of 3-dimensional space and of linear-flowing time are limited to our ordinary experience of the physical world and are invalid when our experience is extended.

The Eastern mystics have long declared that in higher states of consciousness there is a radically different experience of space and time. Not only does one go beyond ordinary 3-dimensional space, but our ordinary awareness of time is also transcended. *Instead of a linear succession of instants or moments of time, one experiences an infinite, timeless and yet dynamic present.* This has been referred to as the 'eternal now'. In this state of consciousness, there is no past, present or future time. They have contracted themselves into a single moment of the present, and this present moment is not something standing still with all its contents, for it ceaselessly moves on.

"In relation to the present do the past and future stand. Even they are present while they last. The present is one alone. Without knowing the truth of the present, seeking to know the past and the future is like wanting to count without the unit, one." (Ramana Maharshi - Verse 15. Forty Verses on Reality)

The Unreality of Space and Time

Quantum field theory postulates that in the sub-atomic world, all collisions (interactions between particles) involve the creation and destruction of particles (electrons, positrons and photons). It also asserts that for every particle there is an anti-particle with equal mass but an opposite charge. The photon, having no charge, is its own anti-particle. This theory has provided a framework for the construction of what are known as 'space-time' diagrams. These depict pictorially the interaction processes observed between particles. Corresponding mathematical expressions express the probability of a process to occur.

The relativistic theory of particle interactions has shown that for every process there is an equivalent process with the direction of time reversed and particles replaced by anti-particles. Particle interactions therefore exhibit a complete symmetry with regard to the direction of time. *All particles can move backward or forwards in time, just as they can move left or right in space.* The concept of a one-way flow of time is therefore not imposed in the interpretation of the space-time diagrams. Space-time diagrams are consequently not seen as chronological records of the path of particles through time, but rather as 4-dimensional patterns in 'space-time', representing a network of inter-related events with no definite direction of time.

The full meaning of 'space-time' in relativistic physics is that time and space are fully equivalent. They are unified into a 4-dimensional continuum ('space-time') in which particle interactions can stretch in any direction of space or time. Particle interactions can therefore only be truly pictured in one '4-dimensional snap-shot' covering the whole of space, as well as the whole region of time. The concept of lapse of time is transcended.

"In 'space-time' therefore, everything that for each of us constitutes the past, the present and the future is given 'en-bloc'. Each observer, as his time passes, discovers - so to

speak - new slices of 'space-time' which appear to his understanding as successive aspects of a material world But, in reality, the entire ensemble of events constituting 'space-time' exists prior to his knowledge of them." [10]

The illusion of a linear flow of time is created because we are unable to see the entire span of time. Our mind can only comprehend time as divided into past, present and future since we perceive only 'cross sections' of the total space-time continuum, one by one, and relate them to the present moment. The illusion of time sequence is thus created.

"The space-time continuum of modern physics represents a plane of consciousness beyond the ordinary physical plane. It permeates space and time on this plane – forming a continuum with all things and beings." [11]

"If one could see the full space-time continuum, we would see all - the past, present and future - with one glance." [12]

The 'space-time' diagrams of quantum field theory are indeed a good representation of the space-time experience of the mystics, in which space and time are integrated as a living continuum. According to the mystics, thought takes place in the linear time of ordinary experience, but their transcendental experience is bound up with space of a higher dimension that is timeless. *This space-time continuum is not demonstrable by science through its investigative methods, but it is experienced by the mystic through various spiritual disciplines that enable him to transcend the plane of his 'relative' existence in space and time.* The four-dimensional 'space-time' of relativistic physics is a similar timeless space of a higher dimension. All events in it, i.e. particle interactions, are interconnected, but the connections are not causal since time does not flow in the full 4-dimensional span of 'space-time', and so there is no 'before' or 'after'. *Time stays just where it is, and it only appears to pass.*

The Unreality of Space and Time

Particle interactions are interpreted in terms of cause and effect only when 'space-time' diagrams are read in a definite time direction. But when they are taken as 4-dimensional patterns without any direction of time attached to them, there is no 'before' or 'after', and therefore no causation. **Causation - like our notions of space and time - is also merely an idea that is limited to our ordinary experience of the world and has to be abandoned when this experience is transcended.** Similarly, the mystics also assert that in transcending time they transcend the world of cause and effect.

According to Advaita Vedanta, the concept of causality is riddled with contradictions. If we postulate a first cause, it implies a beginning for the causal series. This is an arbitrary assumption. On the other hand, if there is no first cause, the causal explanation is incomplete. The first cause must have a previous cause or else the whole causal scheme is illogical. The concept of causality arises because it is rooted in the very organization of our intellect. We are obliged by the nature of our intellect to think in terms of causality i.e. determination of events by antecedent ones. To do so, we break up into past, present and future what comes to us as an unbroken stream i.e. a continuum. Just as diversity is merely an appearance in an undifferentiated indivisible reality, so also are cause and effect. Relationship between events, change and causation are only appearances in reality. Both Gaudapada and Sankara, the foremost exponents of Advaita, assert that since reality cannot be subject to change, the cause (Reality or Brahman) and the effect (the universe) are identical. The universe is therefore only an appearance in reality. Causality, like plurality, is an illusion that pertains to the world of everyday experience, but it does not pertain to reality. It is merely an assumption of science and commonsense.

"Cause and effect are relative, sustaining each other and falling together. Causality is not of the nature of reality but

only a condition of knowledge. We have to negate causality to reach the real, which transcends the phenomenal." [13]

"Space, time and causation are like a glass through which the Absolute is seen. In the Absolute, there is neither space, time nor causation." [14]

"When we refer to the universe, we only mean that perception of existence which is given to us by our mind on the evidence of the senses, and characterized by space, time and causation. Universal scientific laws apply only to this conditioned universe. But beyond it, Existence is not subject to law because space, time and causation do not extend beyond the world of our minds" [15]

CHAPTER 4

THE UNIVERSE AND REALITY

The central aim of Eastern mysticism is to experience the Reality - often referred to as Brahman or the Self - as the sole Existence, and therefore the substratum of the universe. All phenomena in the world appearance - the things and events we observe - will then be experienced merely as manifestations of, and not apart from, the one ultimate Reality. **The Eastern spiritual traditions therefore seek to show their followers various ways of going beyond the ordinary experience of time and space, and thereby gain the realization that the multiplicity of the world appearance - including our own sense of being as separate individuals - is only a manifestation of the underlying Reality.**

The teaching of the sage Sri Ramana Maharshi, as that of all sages, consistently emphasized that Brahman (the Self) - an indivisible unity - was the sole existence and reality; and that 'individual beings' and the 'world' were merely appearances, not apart from this reality, which was their substratum. The ego (individualized consciousness; the notion of individual being; or the 'I' thought) was the cause of the false knowledge that the pluralistic world appearance was real. His unique teaching was the spiritual path of 'self inquiry' by which the truth of the universe - as pure, indivisible Being-Awareness - could be realized by anyone, through inquiry into the nature and source of the ego. Upon such enquiry, the mental tendencies that cause the ego sense or 'I' thought to rise would be gradually weakened, resulting ultimately in its merging into its source - Brahman. With its disappearance, the false knowledge that the world was real, as such, would cease and the universe would be experienced directly, as it really is viz. as formless, eternal, and infinite Existence - Awareness.

"To those who have not realized, as well as to those who have realized, the world is real. To those who have not realized, reality is of the measure of the world. The reality, to those who have realized, is however formless and shines as the ground of the world. This is the difference between the two." (Verse 18. Forty Verses on Reality)

"To those who have not realized the self and to those who have realized it, the body is 'I'. To those who have not realized, the 'I' is only of the measure of the body. But to those who have, within the body, realized the self, the 'I' shines without limit. This is the difference between the two." (Verse 17. Forty Verses on Reality)

"Within us is the body. He who thinks that he is the body makes the same mistake as he who takes the piece of cloth shown in the picture for the screen on which the picture is projected." (Guru Vachaka Kovai Saying 262)

The absolute philosophical standard of reality is continuous, immutable and independent existence, without any intermission or change. For these requirements to be met, reality cannot be in space or time, because things that are in space and time are divisible into parts, and so subject to change. Whatever is real cannot also be related to anything else as cause or effect, since it would then not be changeless. The physical world that we perceive does not meet these standards of reality. The sages thus declare it to be unreal as world, though real as its substratum, - the unchanging, eternal and infinite reality of Existence-Consciousness. **The world, as such, has no existence of its own and is nothing but this Reality all the time.**

"The world and the mind rise and set together as one. But of the two, the world owes its appearance to the mind alone. That alone is real in which this (inseparable) pair — the world and *the mind - have their risings and settings. That reality is the one infinite Consciousness, having neither rising nor setting."* (Verse 7. Forty Verses on Reality)

When the mind is lost in sleep, there is no world appearance. If the world were real however, it should not cease to appear in sleep for two reasons. First, since one's Self has continuous existence throughout the states of waking, dream and deep sleep. Second, since it is of the nature of Pure Awareness, it does not need any medium - mind or senses - to see whatever is real. *The power of the Self of being aware of anything real is never lost. We do not see the world in sleep because the world does not exist as such.* The truth is that the mind, by its own power of self-deception, creates an imaginary world corresponding to its sensations and projects it into an 'outside' which is also its creation. This is what happens in dreams. The processes of creation and projection are unconscious acts, and hence the mind does not question the existence of an 'outside' and of an objective world therein.

The world is unreal. It is nothing but the five kinds of sensations. Of these, the sensation of form is the most important because it is the primary cause of our subjection to the ego sense and our deception by its corollary, the primary ignorance. The ego sense comes into being by taking hold of a form - the body; confounding that form with its true nature as the real Self; and by doing so, limiting the real Self. Identifying with the body, it sees with the physical eye, and therefore sees a physical world of forms that it takes to be real.

When the eye is itself a form, it can only see forms. But neither the physical eye nor the mind has any power of vision of its own. This power is derived from the real eye - our true Self, the formless, pure and infinite Consciousness. Being formless, it cannot see forms. **Forms are created by the very act of seeing** Forms thus appear only because one has confounded the real Self with the ego or sense of individual consciousness. The world is really formless, but to experience this truth one must overcome the ego i.e. the limitation of the real Self to the ego self.

"If the self be with form, the world and God would be so too. But if the self is formless, then how and by whom are forms to be seen? Is the spectacle ever otherwise than the seeing eye is? The real Eye is just the real Self. It is infinite Consciousness, formless and worldless." (Verse 4. Forty Verses on Reality)

"The body is of the form of five sheaths. All five are implied in the term 'body' Apart from the body, is there a world? Say, are there people who, without a body, have seen the world." (Verse 5. Forty Verses on Reality)

If one turns aside from the world appearance and seeks him that sees the world, the world and its seer would vanish together and the Self, alone, would remain.

"The world is not other than the body; the body is not other than the mind; the mind is not other than the Primal Awarenessness; the Primal Awareness is not other than Being. That (alone) exists unchanging, in Peace." (Guru Vachaka Kovai. Saying 99)

"On the plane of relativity, a separate being appears to know something apart from itself. There must therefore be a unity between the two and this, the ego, is of the nature of intelligence. It is akin to the seer rather than the seen, since the latter is insentient. Seeking the seer (the ego) until all the seen disappears, the seer becomes more and more subtle until finally the absolute Seer (the Self) alone remains. The process is thus the disappearance of the objective world." (Talks. Number 25)

"Those who, with egos utterly destroyed, behold the truth, experience all the world as mere appearance, for they themselves shine as the infinite space. They stand convinced that all is but the Self; all made up only of Awareness." (Guru Vachaka Kovai Saying 768)

"Following deep contemplation, (that the world is nothing else but Brahman) one must abide in the bliss of 'Brahman', the Absolute. Old tendencies of the mind however rise up and obstruct such abidance. They have as their root, the ego ('I'-thought), which flourishes in the externally directed, and differentiating (individual) consciousness. 'Nidhidhyasana' is the effort to install the mind firmly in the true 'I' (Brahman) until these tendencies are destroyed, and to awaken the true and pure Consciousness that is the nature of Brahman. This awakening is 'nirvikalpa samadhi' – the direct, immediate and clear perception of Brahman – which is, at once, time and space transcending knowledge and experience. The world of forms is then seen as a manifestation of, and not apart from, Brahman. It is therefore rejected as such, but affirmed as nothing else but Brahman." (Talks. Number 349)

"What is real is hidden from us; but what is false is revealed as true." (Yoga Vasishta).

"We are actually experiencing the Reality (all the time); still we do not know it. Is it not a wonder of wonders?" (Talks. Number 146)

"Considering that the primal cause of all the worlds exists unbroken, all have some reality. But when this derivative form is viewed as infinite and eternal, the ground, the whole, Awareness pure, seems to be non-existent, void." (Guru Vachaka Kovai Saying 20)

"The world of trivial names and forms perceived by the five senses is a mere appearance in the Self, Awareness pure. It is the sport of maya, of images projected by the mind – itself a thought arising in Being Awareness." (Guru Vachaka Kovai Saying 22)

"The true Heart, the Self, - which is indefinable as this or that - is, as it were, the mirror in which all things appear; the mere 'I

AM', self shining Being, pure Awareness, space supreme, perfect wholeness, primal stillness." *(Guru Vachaka Kovai Saying 256)*

"That which is eternal and ever present is not known because of ignorance. This ignorance is identical with the 'I'-thought. It is this thought that obstructs experience of the true 'I' - the Self or 'Brahman' - and true knowledge." *(Talks. Number 197)*

"There is the Absolute Self from which a spark - the ego or 'I' thought - proceeds as from a fire. In the 'ajnani' it immediately identifies with the body and this is ignorance. If this objectifying tendency is killed, it remains pure and merges in its source - Brahman." *(Talks Number 286)*

"Although the awareness (that is a property) of the Self is always present, it is not inimical to ignorance. For ignorance to be destroyed, the subtlest state of mind must be reached by meditation. This subtle state of mind is the natural state of the mind. All other states are modes where it is transformed into forms." *(Talks. Number 624)*

"Scriptural or scientific theories cannot reach finality because Brahman is subtler than the subtlest that can be perceived by the mind. Conceptions are contained within the finite mind whereas the Self (Brahman) is infinite. One must therefore transcend the mind to know the Self. Philosophical or scientific theories are only logical explanations to satisfy the mind. Why look outwards and go on explaining phenomena that are endless when, upon finding the seer, all phenomena are comprised in Him." *(Talks. Number 388)*

"Ignorance or 'avidya' is forgetfulness of one's true being. It follows from the error of confounding one's true being (the Self) with the body - resulting in the 'I am the body' notion. The Self is objectified. This in turn leads to one's notion that the world is indeed real." *(Talks Number 95)*

"From your true being as Awareness, alienated and deluded, do not pursue false appearances - deeming them as real. They are false, since disappear they must. But your own being as Awareness is real and cannot cease to be." (Guru Vachaka Kovai Saying 25)

"Forgetting our true nature as the Reality or Self, we are now obsessed with unrealities, i.e. thoughts and activities. Bhakti (devotion), japa (incantation of names of God) and vichara (self-inquiry) are only different forms of effort to keep out these unrealities, and thus lead us to our true nature. They remove the obstacles standing in the way of revelation of our true being." (Talks Number 401)

"The 'I' thought or ego is the sense of individual existence, whereas the true 'I' is the Self. It is because we exist (as the Self) that the ego also appears to exist. The goal of spiritual endeavour - the Self - thus exists prior to the birth of the ego (upon waking). It is thought, arising following the birth of the ego, that stands between us and our knowing our true nature as the Self." (Talks Number 146)

"The Self alone is the true Eye. Only of the Self does one have direct immediate knowledge. But minds averted from the Self look through the senses at a world other than the Self and think it can be known directly." (Guru Vachaka Kovai saying 878)

"The biblical statement 'Be still and know that I am God' describes realization. To be still is not to think, while knowing means experiencing, not thinking." (Talks Number 131)

"When we, with mind serene and still, experience pure unbroken Being, that state is 'samadhi'. In this state, the mind, abiding as the Self supreme, shares God's own being." (Guru Vachaka Kovai Saying 898)

"Everyone is aware of their existence. 'I am'. There is however the confusion that 'I' is the body because the ego rises from the Absolute Consciousness and gives rise to the intellect. To the intellect, the body is 'I'. If one transcends this false conception, one discovers the true 'I'. This is realization. The Self then remains - as in the sleep state -without perception of a body or a world." (Talks Number 54)

"There is no seen without the seer. The seen therefore has no existence independent of the seer. Consequently, if one understands the seer, one will truly understand the world seen by him." (Talks. Number 387)

"The direct way to solve the question of whether the world is real is to see if the world is really there. Admitting the existence of the world, one must admit the existence of a seer who is none other than one's self. One must find this self to know the relation between the world and its seer. When one seeks the self and abides in its source (the true Self), there is no world to be seen. So what is the reality? It is the seer (the true Self) and not the world. Such being the truth, one continues to argue on the basis that the world is real. Who asked us to accept a brief for the world? Liberation is therefore the abandonment of the false and remaining as Being." (Talks. Number 442)

"After experience of the 'samadhi' state, the world will be taken only at its true worth i.e. merely as a manifestation of the One Reality. World phenomena, being illusory, will leave one unaffected." (Talks. Number 465)

"Just as in dream, one creates a subtle body and world, in the waking state one creates a material body and perceives a material world. In both cases they are creations of the mind. In reality, one is unchanging and continuous. Being that remains in both states, and the phenomena appear on our being like pictures on a screen." (Talks. Number 653)

"One cannot deny one's existence at any moment because one must be there to make the denial. This pure existence is known by stilling the mind, which is naturally outgoing. It is stilled by turning it within. Then the 'I am' - the true Self – or reality prevails alone." (Talks Number 503)

"Following discarding of the physical body and the mind as the real 'I', self analysis should lead to the conclusion that the ego or sense of individuality of a person operates as the perceiver of the existence and sequence of thoughts. Enquiring into the origin of the ego, - the 'I' of the waking state - one argues that if it originated from sleep it was covered up by ignorance, since it was not aware in that state. Such an 'I' (subject to ignorance) cannot be what the sages have affirmed as the true 'I'. So the true 'I' must be beyond sleep and present all along, in the three states of sleep, dream and waking, but without the qualities of these states. It must be the unqualified substratum underlying these states." (Talks. Number 25)

"The world is a superimposition on the one Reality, like the appearance of a snake in a coiled rope in dim light. Because it continues to be seen even after it is known to be unreal, a better analogy is a mirage. The reality of the world in the waking state is no greater than the reality of the dream world during sleep. Either state is unreal when looked at from the other state but real so long as one is in that particular state. The true reality - always real - is the eternal Reality that underlies all three states viz. waking, dream and deep sleep." (Talks Number 399)

"The intellect derives its light (awareness) from the Self. How can the limited and reflected light of the intellect envisage the whole and original Light? The intellect cannot therefore reach or ascertain the nature of the Self." (Talks Number 63)

"If the Self is realized, there is an end to all discourses and disputes. To lead to such realization is the true purpose for which the intellect was developed, but the intellect of man

delights in investigating the causes of effects in the perceived world and speculating about the past and the future. This is because it would lose itself if it turned inwards and searched for the real self." (Talks Number 644)

"The existence of the world is only an impression of the perceiver - the 'rising consciousness' or ego. The 'Being consciousness' - eternal and pure - is always present. The world is the result of the ego and its expansion - the mind - and so one must know the ego to know the true nature of the world. It is then seen to be not different from one's true self." (Talks Number 53)

"There is only the Self. The Self and Pure Consciousness are the same. The world appears to the individual because of his individualized consciousness, of which the source (and substratum) is the Self. What appears is also the Self because there is nothing apart from the Self. As one is also the Self, the perceived is truly within oneself, not outside." (Talks Number 420)

"One is always, and therefore already, the Self - the Eternal Reality. It is only by holding on to this eternal reality that one can realize the transitory nature of the world appearance." (Talks Number 351)

The ultimate Reality - according to Vedic philosophy - is Brahman, which is of the nature of 'Being-Awareness-Bliss'. It is its very nature to manifest itself in myriad forms that come into being and disintegrate, transforming themselves into one another without end. It is seen as intrinsically active and dynamic. The Upanishads thus refer to the Reality as 'unformed, eternal, moving i.e. transcending form but in motion'. The Rig Veda refers to the 'dynamic principle' which is inherent in the universe. The cosmic order is thus given a dynamic connotation.

The Universe and Reality

Vedanta declares that the universe has neither beginning nor end. It manifests in an endless chain of cycles of involution and evolution. At the beginning of each cycle, the First Cause brings forth the universe by a process of expansion - evolution, while at the end of each cycle the universe goes back to the First Cause by a process of contraction - involution.

"That out of which all beings are born; by which they are sustained; and into which they return - That is Brahman, the Supreme." (Taittiriya Upanishad 3- 1)

"Brahman is the One by which the universe is created, sustained and dissolved." (Brahma Sutras 1-1-2)

At the starting point of each cycle, Brahman (the First Cause) is described as 'nirguna' Brahman or as the Transcendent Reality - attribute-less, and beyond both 'being' and 'non-being'. In this un-manifest state, **Brahman is visualized as undifferentiated existence - a state of most intense density in which effects have not manifested, and therefore in which 'cause' is unthinkable.** Nirguna Brahman is neither emptiness nor nothingness, but it holds within itself the forces of attraction, repulsion and harmonization in perfect equilibrium. Modern physics now holds a similar view.

"Our universe must have originated from a source of unimaginably densely concentrated matter in which all the galaxies were packed together within a pinpoint at a definite epoch of time some billions of years ago." [16]

According to the Vedas, creation of the universe begins with the un-manifest Brahman awakening itself into the awareness 'I AM', like the dawn becoming manifest by its own light. This Self Awareness is the basis of the universe - its underlying reality and causeless cause. Brahman, having awakened as the awareness 'I AM', willed that It should manifest itself, resulting in the creative forces which make the One Being evolve into the manifold universe.

"That Being willed 'May I become many; may I grow forth'."
(Chandogya Upanishad)

The universe is therefore seen, not as a creation, but as a manifestation or projection of Brahman itself, by itself and for itself. **The universe has Brahman both as its instrumental as well as its material cause. It is Brahman itself. Brahman - the Reality - unfolds the universe, of its own free will, on the screen of its own Consciousness or Self Awareness.** It is because this Self Awareness is inherent in 'all' its manifestations viz. the forms of the universe as well as the observing mind, that the objective universe is experienced by the observing mind. Thus the Vedic view of the universe provides the common factor between the observer and the observed, and thereby provides a scientific basis for the principle of a 'participatory universe' that has recently emerged in modern physics.

The basic thesis of the Vedas is that there is a Conscious, Supreme Intelligent Reality that is the cause of the cosmos. The order and harmony manifest in the cosmos is explained by this thesis of a Consciousness or Intelligence as its cause, since order and harmony imply the existence of intelligence and design. *As a result of the recent discoveries made in subatomic physics, modern science is also now coming round to the Vedic view of a Conscious Reality as the basis of the universe - abandoning its earlier mechanistic theory of the universe being constituted from ultimate 'building blocks'.*

"The void-like background from which the universe has arisen is not emptiness but a creative potentiality. It is however beyond the reach of science." [17]

The distinguished scientist Carl Jung introduced the concept of a collective consciousness, regarding it as a higher dimension of reality beyond time and space. *Many scientists now concede that the plan and design seen in the universe reveal an astounding principle of order and organization, integration and harmony that can be rationally explained only on the basis of an Intelligent Power.*

The Vedas have personified Brahman as a personal Supreme Being - Ishvara - to account for both creation of the world and the presence of an inherent intelligence in all matter. Ishvara is not Pure Consciousness as is Brahman, but an infinite self-conscious personality. The concept of Ishvara brings the notion of an infinite Brahman - of the nature of pure and infinite consciousness - within the realm and terms of comprehension of the human mind. He is portrayed as the Supreme Intelligent Power responsible for the creation of the universe, its design and organization. *The universe is alive since it is animated from within by Ishvara - all knowing, all pervasive and possessed of all powers. The life of Ishvara throbs in all parts, unifying and containing all.*

Ishvara is thus a mediating principle between Brahman and the world - sharing in the nature of both. He is one with Brahman but yet related to the material world. We thus have in Ishvara the ultimate spirit (Brahman) viewed as ego and endowed with personality, - contemplating the non-ego (universe) as object. Just as our individual egos contemplate their respective worlds as objects, so does Ishvara contemplate the universe.

"For Ishvara, changelessness and inactivity are impossible. As real in the empirical sense, He must be ever-acting, losing himself to find himself, going out to the universe and returning to Himself through the universe." [18]

At a deeper philosophical level, Ishvara and the world - the cause and the effect - are regarded as identical. They are identical, not in the sense of forms or modifications, but in their fundamental nature as Brahman. By the specific quality of his nature, Ishvara transforms himself into the universe. Creation is thus the expression on the plane of space and time of what eternally exists in Brahman.

As the completeness and perfection of Ishvara preclude attribution of any motive for his activity in the creation, design and functioning of the universe, the Vedas assert that the activity of Ishvara is a cosmic game or 'lila' proceeding from his own nature without reference to any purpose.

In Hinduism, the universe has been pictured as a cosmic dance of creation, preservation and destruction involving the various energies that comprise Cosmic Energy. This is symbolized in the Dance of Shiva. The flawless operation of the various laws governing action, reaction and behaviour in the universe is ascribed to the Cosmic Intelligence which projects and executes these laws under one supreme law - the Cosmic Will. This Cosmic Will embodies the complete plan and design of the universe.

Vedic philosophy has invoked the concept of a dynamic Consciousness - 'Akasa'- as the basis of the universe. This concept finds a close counterpart in a very recent concept of modern physics viz. a boundless energy field that forms the basis of the universe.

"The 'akasa' which is potential Consciousness and the primal form of matter vibrates under the influence of 'prana' which is the Vital Energy and the source of all the energies in the cosmos. When the vibration becomes quicker, the 'akasa' is lashed into all the diverse wave forms that create the universe." (Kathopanishad 11-6-2)

This Vedic picture of a dynamic universe is closely approached by discoveries in sub-atomic physics which have demonstrated that the 'particles' that constitute the material phenomena in the world materialize spontaneously out of a formless 'void' and vanish again into the 'void'. **Both the Vedas and modern physics thus see the multiplicity of objects or forms constituting the world appearance as being, in truth, only modifications of a formless Cosmic Consciousness-Energy** principle into gross forms. The human mind however - on the evidence of the senses - regards them as real as it cannot experience the very subtle Consciousness-Energy principle - the Reality beyond.

"Akasa is the ultimate source and basis of all things and beings." (Chandogya Upanishad)

"Akasa is a living void, pulsating in endless rhythms of creation, preservation and destruction." [19]

In yet another symbolism of the dynamic nature of the universe, Vedic philosophy has invoked two principles - 'Shiva' and 'Shakti'. 'Shiva' is described as the guiding Consciousness, while 'Shakti' is his dynamic working power or energy. Here Shiva represents the changeless and stable potential, while Shakti represents the creative power behind movement and change. The two principles complement and interact with each other - resulting in the manifestation of the material universe.

"Shiva is the One who inheres in all things. He is all that is." (Svetasvatara Upanishad)

"Shakti is the Inexhaustible Reservoir of Energies - creating and manifesting in all objects and phenomena." (Devi Bhagavata 11-12-21)

"Siva (as Supreme Awareness-Being) alone abides - the ground, the screen. The world of triads is but the picture on the screen - the play of Sakti (as Supreme Awareness-Active)." (Guru Vachaka Kovai Saying 43)

"Those who have sought and gained the goal of true Awareness do not see the world as variegated forms. The whole world filled with crowds of objects is for them but the gracious play of one sole Sakti, one sole power - the power of pure Awareness." (Guru Vachaka Kovai saying 58)

The general picture emerging from the Vedas is therefore of an organic, rhythmically moving universe in which everything is ever changing. As the Bhagavad Gita says, 'All activity takes place by the interweaving of forces inherent in Nature'. The world of ceaseless change is thus called 'samsara', which literally translated means incessant motion. All static forms are regarded as illusory, and are explained on the basis of the two philosophical concepts of 'avidya' and 'maya'.

According to the philosophy of Advaita Vedanta, the phenomenal appearance of the world cannot be regarded as real; so this appearance is regarded as 'maya' or appearance of Reality. *The innermost self or essence of the world is Brahman, and if it seems to be independent of Brahman, then it is not what it seems to be. In this sense, the term 'maya' signifies an illusory or deceptive appearance of the real.* Brahman and the world are one and co-exist as reality and appearance. The finite world is the infinite Brahman, but the infinite Brahman is hidden from our view. The world is regarded as 'maya' because it is a deceptive appearance and not the essential truth of the reality of Brahman.

Every logical attempt to relate Brahman to the world of experience ends in failure. Though the world hangs on Brahman, it does not affect Brahman. It is a case of causality where the cause produces an effect without undergoing any change. **The relation of the finite world to the infinite Brahman is a mystery for human understanding.** According to Advaita Vedanta, while Brahman is the basis of the world, Brahman is, and is not, identical with the world. It is, because the world is not apart from Brahman. It is not, because Brahman is not subject to the changes of the world. *The term 'maya' has also been used, in a somewhat different sense to that in the previous paragraph, to signify this mystery as to how Brahman appears to us as the world.*

Yet another connotation of the term 'maya' envisaged in Advaita is that it the inherent energy or 'finitising' principle present in the Supreme Being by which its potential for manifestation as forms is transformed into the pluralistic world appearance. Its presence in the Supreme is inferred from its effects. The forms of the world, in their un-evolved condition, inhere in the Supreme and in their developed state constitute the world.

In the philosophy of Advaita Vedanta, the cause of our perception of a pluralistic world is in the nature of our intellect and not in Brahman, which is a unity and indivisible. The nature of Brahman - the Reality - is beyond sensory perception, but the intellect bases its perceptions on the evidence of the senses. It therefore tends to confuse the perceived, illusory and empirical universe for the transcendental reality of Brahman, which is its substratum. This natural tendency of the intellect is ascribed to an inexplicable power of Brahman called 'avidya'. *It is a natural obscuration of our knowledge due to the nature of the finite intellect that makes it impossible for it to perceive except through the senses and the texture of space, time and cause. We cannot know the true nature of reality so long as we are subject to the logical mode of thinking of the finite mind, or 'avidya'.* It shuts us off from true knowledge of our own reality and that of the world Advaita Vedanta therefore asserts that when 'avidya' is overcome, the appearance of the world will vanish. The appearance then stands transfigured in the Absolute.

The doctrine of 'avidya' (which translates as false knowledge) may suggest a misleading view that nothing exists and that the phenomenal world is purely illusory i.e. in the nature of a dream. Sankara however makes it clear that there is a Reality underlying the appearance of the world. The world is therefore unreal as such, - like the unreality of a mirage - but it is not illusory in the sense of non-being or a dream, as it has the Real for a basis. According to Advaita, we are able to penetrate to the Real through the world - in the intuitive experience of Brahman - precisely because this world of appearance bears within it the Real. What is based on the real and not the real itself can only be regarded as an appearance of the real. **The world is thus the phenomenal truth of Brahman but not its essential truth. It is the manner in which we are compelled to see the Real within the limits of our finite consciousness.**

Just as Hinduism and other Eastern religious traditions see the universe as everchanging and rhythmically moving, - a web with dynamic inter-connections, - modern physics has also come to understand the universe as such a dynamic web of relations. The dynamic aspect of matter arises in quantum theory as a consequence of the wave nature of particles - which implies that the 'being' of matter cannot be separated from its activity. The properties of sub-atomic particles can be understood only in a dynamic context i.e. in terms of movement, interaction and transformation. The dynamic nature of the universe also arises in relativity theory through the unification of space and time.

In the vibrating atoms that link up to form the objects of the material world, the electrons are confined to minute volumes by the electric forces that bind them to the nucleus. Similarly, within the nucleus itself, the protons and neutrons are confined to a very minute volume by exceptionally strong nuclear forces. All these particles are thus subject to intense confinement. According to quantum theory, these sub-atomic particles also exist as waves. Because of this feature, they react to their confinement by whirling around. The greater their degree of confinement, the faster their velocities. *This tendency of particles to react to increased confinement with greater motion implies a fundamental 'restlessness' of matter in the sub-atomic world. Macroscopically, the material objects around us seem to be inert, but the closer they are looked at, they are full of activity and alive. Modern physics therefore pictures matter not as passive and inert, but as being in a continuous vibrating and dancing motion. This is similar to how the mystics have always seen the world.*

The Universe and Reality

In physics, the dynamic nature of the universe is also seen in the world of stars. Rotating clouds of hydrogen gas contract to form stars - heating up and becoming burning fires in the sky. They still continue to rotate and material ejected into space spirals outwards, condensing into planets which circle round the star. After millions of years, when the hydrogen fuel has been used up, the star expands and then contracts to collapse.

The stars cluster into galaxies of various shapes that also rotate - the stars moving round the centre of their galaxy. The universe is full of such galaxies, all spinning. Studies of the universe as a whole - at the highest scale of space and time - have thus revealed that the universe is not a static one, but a rhythmically expanding and contracting one - on a vast scale of space and time.

Experiencing the universe as an organic and rhythmically moving cosmos - expanding and contracting on a scale of vast proportions - the Hindu mystics had developed cosmologies that closely parallel those of modern science. *The evolution of the cosmos, as a whole, was described as a rhythmic divine play called 'lila', which goes on in endless cycles. In each cycle the 'One' becomes the many and the many then return into the 'One'.' Each unimaginable span of time between the beginning and end of one cycle was termed a 'kalpa'. It has taken the human mind and scientific progress more than 2000 years to come up with a similar concept of the universe!*

Two fundamental concepts of classical physics are those of energy and mass. Energy is the capacity to do work and is therefore always associated with some process or activity. A fundamental feature of energy is that the total energy involved in a process is always conserved. The form of energy can change, but none of it can get lost. The mass of a body was a measure of the pull of gravity on the body, and also of its inertia or resistance to acceleration. In classical physics, mass was associated with the notion of indestructible material substance and it was believed that mass, like energy, was also rigorously conserved.

Relativity theory has however shown that mass is nothing but a form of energy. It is therefore destructible since it can be transformed into other forms of energy. In sub-atomic collisions for instance, a particle can be destroyed and the energy contained in its mass transformed into kinetic energy. This kinetic energy is then re-distributed amongst the other particles participating in the collision. The kinetic energy of colliding sub-atomic particles can also produce the masses of new particles. The creation and destruction of particles is a consequence of the equivalence of mass and energy. Only the total energy involved in particle collisions i.e. the total kinetic energy plus the energy contained in the masses of all the particles, is conserved.

The mass of a particle is therefore no longer associated with a material substance, and particles are now regarded as bundles of energy. Since energy is however associated with activity or processes, it implies that the nature of particles is intrinsically dynamic. The particles can only be conceived in relativistic terms, i.e. in a framework where space and time are fused into a 4-dimensional continuum. They are 4-dimensional entities in space-time – dynamic patterns that have a space aspect as well as a time aspect. Their space aspect makes them appear as objects with a certain mass, while their time aspect makes them appear as processes involving the equivalent energy.

These dynamic patterns or 'energy bundles' form the stable nuclear, atomic and molecular structures that build up matter and give it its solid appearance. This solid appearance makes us believe that matter is really made up of some material substance. The energy bundles are however dynamic energy patterns changing continually into one another - a continuous dance of energy.

Quantum theory has thus shown particles to be probability patterns, and not isolated grains of solid matter. Particles are depicted as dynamic patterns and as interconnections in an inseparable cosmic web of interactions. The latter involve a ceaseless flow of energy, manifesting as the exchange of particles. Relativity theory, on the other hand, has revealed the intrinsically dynamic nature of particles viz. that they are processes, and that the activity of matter is the very essence of its being. *The existence of matter and its activity are inseparable. They are but different aspects of the same multi-dimensional space-time reality.*

Awareness of such a Reality, in a non-ordinary state of consciousness, had led mystics to the dynamic worldview now held in modern physics - where the particles of the sub-atomic world are seen in terms of energy, activity and processes. **All objects are now seen - both by mystics and modern physicists - as processes in universal flux; there is no material substance; and there is no place for static shapes.** The basic elements of the universe are dynamic patterns in a constant flow of transformation and change. Reality is not found in substance as in classical Western philosophy but in relationships and change - as postulated in the Vedic and other Eastern philosophies.

What is the nature of the world? It is perpetual change, continuous, interminable flux. When you try to get at form, you will find reality only. (Maharshi's Gospel. p 63)

According to Advaita Vedanta, the objects of the world are always changing. They never are, but always become. By definition, reality is eternal and changeless being since nothing that changes is real. The changing world is therefore not real. Advaita sees the world as neither 'pure being' nor 'pure non-being'. Arguing that 'pure being' is not an item of the world process while 'pure non-being' is illogical, it concludes that what exists is 'becoming', which is neither being nor non-being. At no point can the world reach being and stop becoming. The relation of being to non-being in the finite world is not one of exclusion but one of polar opposition. The two are at the same time antithetic and correlative. Neither of them attains actuality except through its contrast with the other. However much the one may penetrate the other or be penetrated by it, the distinction and contrast are always there, so that everything in the world is in a state of change.

Because of the basic interconnectedness of the sub-atomic world, we cannot hope to understand the nature and properties of any one sub-atomic particle without understanding all the others. Sub-atomic physics has therefore sought, in recent years, to work towards a complete understanding through partial theories and models.

CHAPTER 5

THE VOID, FORM AND THE COSMIC DANCE

Gravity is associated with a gravitational field. Such fields are created and felt by all massive bodies. Space around a massive body is 'conditioned' so that another object will feel the gravitational force. The field also manifests itself as a curvature of the space around the body. The two cannot be distinguished because the field itself is the curved space. *In Einstein's theory therefore, not only is matter inseparable from its field of gravity but the field of gravity is also inseparable from the curved space.* **Matter and space are thus inseparable, interdependent parts of a single whole.**

The various kinds of electromagnetic radiation are vibrating electric and magnetic fields that travel through space as waves. In classical electrodynamics, the electric and magnetic fields were regarded as primary physical entities that could be studied without any reference to material bodies. Following the realization that an electric field can also appear as a magnetic field, the two fields were unified into a single electromagnetic field.

The classical theory of electrodynamics has now been combined with quantum theory in a theory called 'quantum electrodynamics'. By combining the two concepts viz. that of electro-magnetic fields and that of photons as particle manifestations of electromagnetic waves, *the theory has shown that the photons - the particle manifestations of electromagnetic waves - must also be manifestations of electromagnetic fields.* **Hence the concept of the 'quantum field' or a field that can take the form of particles, or quanta.** Each type of particle corresponds to a different field. The classical contrast between 'solid' and 'surrounding space' is thus completely overcome.

The quantum field is thus seen as the fundamental physical entity – a continuous medium that is present everywhere in space. Particles are merely local condensations of the field. They are in the nature of concentrations of energy that come and go – losing their individual character and dissolving into the underlying field. Einstein therefore described matter as *'regions of space in which the field is extremely intense.'* According to him, **'physics therefore has no place for both the field and matter because the field is the only reality'.** [20]

"*The field exists everywhere. It is the cause of all phenomena. The 'being' and the 'fading' of particles are merely forms of motion of the field.*" [21]

Emptiness and Form

The classical mechanistic worldview that envisaged solid indestructible particles moving in a void is therefore no longer valid. There is no longer any sharp distinction between particles and space surrounding them. *The particles that constitute the material phenomena of the world materialize spontaneously out of the void and vanish into it again. The void has thus come to be recognized as a dynamic entity and of paramount importance.*

Such a concept, viz. that all physical things and phenomena are transient manifestations of, and in, an underlying fundamental entity has always been held by the Eastern mystics who consider this as the sole Reality, and the manifestations as illusory. This reality of the mystic - which has been called 'Brahman' by the Hindus - does not however correspond to the quantum field of the physicist because it is seen as the essence of all phenomena and therefore beyond all concepts; whereas the quantum field is a well defined concept that accounts for only some of the physical phenomena.

Since this underlying Reality is formless and indescribable, the Eastern mystics have referred to it as 'akasa' – the void or emptiness. But this emptiness does not mean nothingness. On the contrary, it is asserted to be the primal form of matter - the essence of all forms and the source of all life.

"Akasa is the ultimate source and basis of all things and beings." (Chandogya Upanishad)

"This thing here, that there, whatever objects we confront, the true being of them all is the pure, bright space of Awareness shining as the Self." (Guru Vachaka Kovai Saying 1074)

The void is thus seen as having an infinite creative potential. Like the quantum field it gives birth to an infinite variety of forms that it sustains and eventually re-absorbs. The forms or manifestations are dynamic or transitory, with no fundamental reality; the void is one ceaseless dance of movement and energy.

The illusion of a material substance being based on what is really movement finds an analogy in the water wave. The up and down movement of water particles makes us believe that a 'piece' of water is actually moving over the water surface.

Modern physics, which has transferred our gaze from the visible to the underlying 'field' has established that the presence of matter is merely an accidental disturbance of the perfect state of the quantum field at that place. Accordingly, there can be no simple laws to describe forces between elementary particles. Order must be sought in the underlying field.

The quantum field is a continuum present everywhere in space but in its particle aspect it has a discontinuous granular structure.

Quantum field and matter transform themselves endlessly into one another and are merely two aspects of the same reality. Eastern mysticism also emphasizes a similar dynamic unity between the 'Void' and the forms it creates. *This relationship of emptiness and form is viewed not as one of mutually exclusive opposites, but as two co-existing aspects of the same reality.* [22]

The field theories of modern physics conceive the forces between sub-atomic particles in terms of interactions between particles mediated through fields i.e. through other particles. Force is therefore nothing but the macroscopic effect of these particle exchanges. *Force and matter – the two concepts that were so sharply demarcated in Newtonian atomism – are therefore now seen to have their common origin in the dynamic patterns that we call particles. Such a view of force is also found in Eastern mysticism, which regards motion and change as essential and intrinsic properties of all things.*

Particles cannot be separated from the space surrounding them because, on the one hand, they determine the structure of that space; on the other hand, they cannot be regarded as other than condensations of a continuous field that is present throughout space. *This quantum field is seen as the basis of all particles as well as of their mutual interactions. Being and fading of particles are merely forms of motion of the field.*

Advaita Vedanta holds a very similar view since, in the mystic experience, the objects of the world are found to be transient and ever changing. They never 'are' but always 'become' Since the real is what is eternal and unchanging, the changing world is regarded as unreal. What exists is 'becoming', which is neither pure being nor pure non-being. At no point can the world reach being and stop becoming.

According to field theory, virtual particles can come into being spontaneously out of the void and vanish again into the void without any nucleon or other strongly interacting particle being present. The void is thus far from empty. On the contrary, it contains an unlimited number of particles that can come into being and vanish without end. **The void is therefore not a state of mere nothingness, but contains the potentiality for all forms of the particle world. These forms, in turn, are not independent physical entities but merely transient manifestations of the underlying void.**

The relation between the void and the virtual particles is thus dynamic. It is truly a 'living void' pulsating in endless rhythms of creation and destruction. From its role - in classical physics - as an empty container of physical phenomena, the void has emerged as a dynamic entity of the utmost importance. *Modern physics no longer separates the 'being' of matter from its activity. It concedes that a supremely intelligent Consciousness underlies matter at the subatomic level and also subtends the relative plane of space, time and causation This position is very close to the position always held in Vedic philosophy viz. that* **Cosmic Consciousness is the sole reality in the universe.**

"Supreme Infinite Perfect Consciousness (Bhuma) alone exists. From it arises individual finite consciousness by limitation." (Talks Number 68)

"Since that which is continuous is permanent and real, and that which is discontinuous is transitory and unreal, the state of Being-Consciousness is real while the objects of our ego-awareness are unreal." (Talks Number 609)

"Being (Sat) and Consciousness (Chit) are one and the same reality. The reality cannot be one and not the other because the logical conclusions of a contrary view are absurd viz. insentient Being or Consciousness that has no being." (Talks Number 506)

"The world is, in reality spirit (consciousness) alone. Because of our identification with a physical body, the world also appears to be physical. But That which exists is only spirit (consciousness) and will be realized to be so if one realizes that oneself is spirit alone." (Talks Number 328)

"If one with mind turned towards Awareness and concentrating on Awareness seeks the Self, the world made up of ether and other elements is real as all things are (seen as) Awareness - the one sole substance of true Being." (Guru Vachaks Kovai Saying 52)

"Still, waveless Being-Awareness-Bliss alone is what the true seer sees, and is. Since the seer and sight are one, it surely follows that this world is also Being-Awareness-Bliss." (Guru Vachaka Kovai Saying 54)

The views regarding the nature of reality held in science and the spiritual tradition of the East are thus very similar. According to the Vedic philosophy, the whole universe of objects in space came into existence by various processes of 'condensation' of Consciousness into gross forms. **The substance of the universe is consciousness only; and since this consciousness is the one substratum of all objects, beings, events and phenomena, the whole universe has a basic unity However, because of the divine power called 'maya', this universe appears to the human mind as a multiplicity of forms; and this conceals from man the reality of his own 'being' as well as that of the universe that is perceived by him.** The Vedic view, therefore, is that as long as we confuse the world appearance with reality, without perceiving the unity (Brahman) that underlies it, we are under the spell of 'maya'. Maya is the illusion of taking shapes and structures, things and events as realities of nature instead of realizing that they are merely concepts of our measuring and categorizing minds.

The Void, Form and the Cosmic Dance

"All this world of forms is the very stuff of man's mind. It is created and sustained by the energy of thought and thought alone." (Nyaaya Sutra Bashya of Vatsyayana)

Advaita Vedanta holds that the universe is not what it appears to be to man's mind through his senses. This is because sensory perception cognizes only the 'physical world' which exists only as an illusory manifestation of the Absolute Reality that is its substratum. *The deluding principle that masks the reality is called 'maya'.* **Modern physics now holds a similar position since it asserts that this world of space, time and causality has no independent existence and that the reality is its substratum - the void - of infinite potential.**

From the practical standpoint however, one cannot regard the perceived world as an illusion. The world is a creation of the mind (under the influence of 'maya') and thus both stand or fall together. Both are of the same order of reality or unreality. Hindu scriptures exhort us to remember that the world is only relatively true, and that the absolute truth is that all things and beings are Brahman Tentative acceptance of this truth is considered essential if one is to make one's life in this world serve its true purpose viz. realize *by direct experience* that all beings, the world and its creator are really one - the Eternal Consciousness.

The Cosmic Dance

In relativistic theory, particles are not seen as indestructible objects but as dynamic patterns involving a certain amount of energy that can be redistributed when new patterns are formed. Sub-atomic physics has thus revealed the intrinsically dynamic nature of matter. The sub-atomic particles are dynamic patterns that are not isolated entities but integral parts of a unity that is in the nature of a network of interactions. The latter involve a ceaseless flow of energy, manifesting as the exchange of particles. The interactions are a dynamic display in which particles are created and destroyed endlessly in a continuous variation of energy patterns. **The whole universe is thus in endless motion and activity - a continuous dance of energy.**

Astrophysics has shown us that outer space is also filled with electromagnetic radiation of various frequencies i.e. photons of various energies caused by collisions of sub-atomic particles in the centre of the stars. Cosmic radiation also contains massive high-energy particles of various kinds whose origin is unknown. When these high-energy cosmic rays hit the atmosphere of the Earth, collisions between the very high-energy particles and the nuclei of air molecules take place and result in a vast array of secondary particles. These either decay or undergo further collisions – thereby creating more particles that, in turn, decay or collide again. This process goes on until the original kinetic energy is transformed into a shower of particles and thus gradually absorbed. *There is therefore a continual flow of energy in the atmosphere, going through a great variety of particle patterns in a rhythmic dance of creation and destruction.*

Modern physics has thus shown us that movement and rhythm are essential properties of matter; and that all matter, whether here on Earth or in outer space, is involved in a continual 'cosmic dance'. **This metaphor of a cosmic dance is beautifully expressed in Hinduism in the image of the dance of Shiva. The dance symbolizes the direct experience of the mystics that the universe and all life are part of a great rhythmic process of creation and destruction that goes on in endless cycles.** The dance involves the various energies that comprise the Cosmic Energy. The dancing Shiva is a depiction of the supreme truth that the manifold forms of the world are 'maya'; they are not fundamental but illusory and always changing, as Lord Shiva keeps creating and dissolving them in the ceaseless flow of his dance.

As the dancing Shiva is a personification of Brahman, the activity is that of Brahman's myriad manifestations as the world appearance. **The dance is the dancing universe - the ceaseless flow of energy going through an infinite variety of patterns that melt into one another.**

"The moment an atom perishes, that moment a fresh atom comes into existence. Incessantly this happens and it looks as if it happened of its own accord." (Guru Vachaka Kovai Saying 667)

The description in Advaita Vedanta of 'maya' as the energy of Ishvara - the inherent power by which he transforms the potential for forms into the actual world of forms - is in accordance with this view of a cosmic dance of energy. The presence of 'maya' is inferred from its effects.

"The names and forms, in their un-evolved condition, inhere in Ishvara and in their developed state constitute the world." [23]

Modern physics has shown that the rhythm of creation and destruction is the very essence of matter since, according to quantum field theory; all interactions between particles take place through the emission and absorption of particles. More than that, it has shown that *the dance of creation and destruction is the very basis of the existence of matter since all particles self-interact by emitting and re-absorbing virtual particles.* **Every sub-atomic particle not only performs an energy dance, but also is itself an energy dance – a pulsating process of creation and destruction.**

The patterns of this dance are an essential aspect of the nature of each particle and determine many of its properties. Also, since virtual particles are not only an essential part of all particle interactions and of most particles' properties but are also created and destroyed by the void, *both matter and the void participate in the cosmic dance – creating and destroying energy patterns without end.*

For modern physics therefore, Shiva's dance corresponds to the dance of sub-atomic matter. It is a continuous dance of creation and destruction involving the whole cosmos. It is thus the basis of all existence and of all phenomena. Bubble chamber photographs of interacting particles - showing the continual rhythm of creation and destruction - are therefore visual images of the dance of Shiva produced by modern science.

CHAPTER 6

PATTERNS IN STRUCTURE AND CHANGE

The sub-atomic world is seen by modern physics as one of rhythm, motion and change. It is however not a random world without order. There are definite patterns. The patterns that have emerged in the sub-atomic world are very similar to those of the world of atoms. Thus, as in the case of atoms, all strongly interacting particles (called hadrons) fall into sequences, the members of which differ only in their masses and spins. Again, as in the case of atoms, the higher members of a hadron sequence are not seen as different particles but merely as differently excited states of the member with the lowest mass and spin. Like atoms, hadrons too apparently exist in short lived quantum states in respect of mass and spin. *These similarities between the quantum states of atoms and hadrons suggest that the latter too, like atoms, have internal structures that are capable of being excited i.e. capable of absorbing energy to form a variety of patterns.*

All attempts to break up hadrons into constituent particles have however failed, despite the very high energies used. The fragments resulting from collisions were never smaller fragments but entire new hadrons formed out of the kinetic energies and masses of the colliding hadrons.

"The decomposition of a sub-atomic particle - far from being a definite process - depends on the energy involved in the collision process. It is a situation where dynamic energy patterns are dissolved and rearranged. The classical notion of composite structures made up of component parts is no longer applicable. **The structure of the particle can only be**

understood in a dynamic sense i.e. in terms of processes, patterns and interactions."[24]

S-Matrix Theory

The discovery of patterns in the particle world led physicists subscribing to the mechanistic worldview to believe that these patterns were the result of 'fundamental symmetries' being expressed as fundamental laws of nature. **Modern physics has however gone beyond the view that particle patterns are the result of fundamental laws of nature and shown that they are the consequence of the dynamic nature and essential inter-relatedness of the subatomic world.** The concept of symmetry is seen as a construct of the human mind rather than a property of nature. The search for fundamental symmetries in the realm of particle physics is apparently rooted in the Hellenic heritage of the West, which accorded symmetry and geometry a central role in both science and philosophy.

Recent research in particle physics has indicated that the patterns and regularities observed in particle structure can be theoretically represented in a simple way through a model based on the assumption that all hadrons are made up of elementary particles called 'quarks'. So far however, all attempts to break up hadrons into such constituent particles have failed despite the very high energies used. As indicated earlier, the fragments resulting from the collisions were always entire new hadrons - formed out of the kinetic energies and masses of the colliding hadrons.

The existence of quarks as physical constituents of hadrons also runs up against severe theoretical difficulties. Since forces in the particle world involve other particles, it implies that the postulated quarks must also have an internal structure. But this contradicts the very basis of the quark model, which postulates that quarks are structure-less and point-like. *There is therefore a paradoxical situation in that hadrons behave as though they were composed of point-like elementary constituents (the so-called quarks); but the physical existence of such constituents (the quarks) is precluded by the present state of knowledge of particles and their interactions.*

The paradox has been resolved by a new theoretical framework that views structure in the sub-atomic world in dynamic rather than static terms. Particle patterns are regarded, not as fundamental features of nature, but rather as a consequence of the dynamic and essentially inter-related nature of the subatomic world. The new framework, called S-matrix theory, was developed by Heisenberg, one of the most outstanding physicists of our times. The S-matrix is a collection of the probabilities for all possible interactions involving hadrons. The interactions are represented symbolically by S-matrix diagrams.

The important new concept in S-matrix theory is the shift in emphasis from objects to events i.e. from particles to their reactions. It thus accords with quantum theory, which views sub-atomic particles as manifestations of the interactions between the various processes involved in measurement i.e. as events that interconnect other events. It also accords with relativity theory, which conceives of particles in terms of space-time i.e. as 4-dimensional patterns, and as processes rather than as objects. Using the four-dimensional formalism of relativity theory, it describes all the properties of hadrons in terms of reaction possibilities - thereby establishing an intimate link between particles and processes. Each reaction involves particles that link it to other reactions and thus a whole network of processes is built up. *The particle is thus seen as part of a whole network of interactions i.e. as part of a 'tissue of events' all described by the S-matrix.* Each reaction occurs with a certain probability that depends on the available energy and the characteristics of the reaction, and these probabilities are given by the various elements of the S-matrix. [25]

This approach has allowed the structure of a hadron to be defined in a thoroughly dynamic way. *The structure of a hadron is no longer regarded as an arrangement of components, but is determined by all the sets of particles that may interact to form that hadron.* By thus defining the structure of a hadron as its tendency to undergo various reactions, S-matrix theory has given the concept of structure a new and essentially dynamic connotation. Such a notion of structure is in perfect agreement with the observed experimental fact that whenever hadrons are broken up, they disintegrate into combinations of other hadrons. They can be said to 'consist' potentially of these hadron combinations.

In this picture, hadron reactions represent a flow of energy in which particles are created and dissolved. According to the theory, the energy flows only through certain 'reaction channels', each of which contains several 'singularities' which are values of particle energy and momentum where creation of new particles becomes possible. At these values, the mathematical structure of the S-matrix changes abruptly. As the locations of these 'singularities' reflect the properties of the hadrons, and all the hadrons can be created in particle interactions, the 'singularities' of the S-matrix mirror all the patterns and symmetries of hadrons. [26]

This view of hadrons as being intermediate states in a network of reactions requires that we must be able to explain the forces through which they interact. These are the strong interaction forces between hadrons. They 'scatter' colliding hadrons; dissolve them; and rearrange them in new patterns. *The interacting forces are generated by the bound states of the interacting hadrons and therefore are an intrinsic property of these particles.* Such an understanding of interaction forces also implies that all known particles must have some internal structure since only then can they interact with the observer and thus be susceptible to detection. There can be no truly elementary particle in the sense that there is no internal structure because it would not be subject to any forces that would enable us to infer its existence. The mere knowledge of the existence of a particle thus implies that it has an internal structure. S-matrix theory however indicates that structure can have a dynamic, fluid and subtle connotation rather than the static physical one normally associated with classical physics.

The challenge for S-matrix theory has been to use this dynamic concept of hadrons to account, on the one hand, for the symmetries that give rise to the observed hadron patterns and, on the other, for the laws of conservation of momentum, energy, amount of rotation and electric charge that govern all hadron interactions. Hadron symmetries must be reflected in the mathematical structure of the S-matrix in such a way that the matrix contains only those elements that correspond to reactions allowed by the laws of conservation. The laws would then be the consequence of S-matrix structure and thus a consequence of the dynamic nature of hadrons. [27]

Physicists have been trying to arrive at such a mathematical structure of the S-matrix by postulating general principles that would restrict the mathematical possibilities for constructing S-matrix elements. This would give the S-matrix a definite structure. Three general principles have been established and the central aim of S-matrix theory is to derive the singularity structure of the S-matrix from these principles. These general principles are the basis of our scientific methods of observation and measurement i.e. of the scientific framework. Up to now, it has not been possible to construct a mathematical model that satisfies all three principles, but the leading physicists in this field expect that, with future research, they will be sufficient to determine all the properties of the S-matrix - and thus all the properties of hadrons - uniquely. If this turns out to be the case, the philosophical implications would be very profound, since these general principles form the basis of our scientific methods of observation and measurement. *If they suffice to determine hadron structure, it means that* **the basic structures of the physical world are determined, ultimately, by the way we look at this world.** *Any fundamental change in our* *observational methods would imply a modification of the general principles - leading to a different structure of the S-matrix and thus a different structure of hadrons. It means, ultimately, that the structure and phenomena that we observe in nature are nothing but the creations of our measuring and categorizing minds. It also reflects the* **impossibility of separating the** *scientific* **observer** *from* **the observed phenomena** [28]

States of Consciousness in Relation to Reality

These conclusions - implied by S-matrix theory - coincide with the teachings of Vedic philosophy. **Hindu mystics have always maintained the view that all the things and events we perceive are mere creations of our mind. They arise from a particular state of consciousness, and dissolve when this state is transcended.** Vedic philosophy thus deals with the states of dream and dreamless sleep in addition to that of waking, with which alone conventional science is concerned. All three are held to represent equally valid, particular states of consciousness and they must all be considered and analyzed if one is to arrive at reality.

"Waking and dream experiences are seen by a seer who is the true 'I' and not the mind. This is deduced from the fact that one's existence is unbroken and continuous throughout all three states. The mind, however, only has intermittent existence. It cannot therefore be one's self or true 'I' (as our existence is unbroken). A proof of one's existence in sleep is our recollection of the sleep experience upon waking. The true 'I' is the one that experiences all the three states but is unaffected by them, just as the screen is not affected by the pictures that appear thereon." (Talks Number 487)

"One is aware of the world in the waking state but not during sleep. When others say that the world existed whilst one was asleep, they are merely testifying to 'their' awareness of the

world in 'their' waking state. Nobody is aware of a world while they are asleep. But all testify to the existence of a world in dream or waking - the reason being that the world is a creation of the mind that rises in these two states. The mind is withdrawn in the state of deep sleep and so there is no world to be seen. It manifests again upon waking when the mind rises again. The seer and experiencer of the world (of waking and dream) is the Self, which is however unaffected." (Talks Number 487)

"Just as in dream, one creates a seer and the surroundings and these are later withdrawn into oneself, so it is in the waking state - the One becoming the many. In both states, the objective world is really subjective – within the observer's mind. How do they exist there? One's awareness of a world is by 'abhasa' or the intermittent reflected light of the permanent Self (which is the original light)." (Talks Number 474)

"The world is only in the mind It does not speak out saying 'I am the world'. If it did, it would have to be always present, even in your sleep. Since it is not present in your sleep, it is impermanent. Being impermanent, it has no reality. The Self alone is permanent (and therefore real)." (Talks. Number 251)

"In deep sleep the world is not and 'I' as body too is not; but the Self, as being, persistent shines. Hence the true 'I', one must agree, is only the immutable Self." (Guru Vachaka Kovai Saying 355)

"It is a false belief that we are part of a world that exists apart from us. In reality the world is within us, in the mind, since we perceive it only in the waking state when the mind has arisen. Since one always exists, even in sleep, one should be aware of the world in sleep too if it existed apart from oneself, since the self (the true infinite 'I') is always aware. When the self identifies itself with the limited false 'I' or ego there is a world. The creation of a subject-object relationship is the creation of the world. Both (the ego and the world) are creations in Pure

Consciousness – the Self (true 'I'). If the subject-object relation is terminated, the Self remains alone." (Talks Number 453)

"A person dreams and then awakes. One's being in the room upon waking, and being in a dream scene during the dream are both unreal (since they are both impermanent). But both appear real to the mind in the waking and dream states respectively. The 'I' of the waking state, and the 'I' that speaks of the dream upon waking, are also both unreal as they too are transient. The substratum of awareness - the Self - that continues unbroken all along and which is the 'canvas' on which all the scenes - in both dream and waking - appear, is the reality." (Talks Number 49)

"Just as the dream world - filled with pleasures and pains - ceases to interest us upon waking, so will the present world of the waking state cease to interest us upon waking into our true natural state, when it is realized that it is not an objective reality but only our thought." (Talks Number 625)

"With the ego half-emerged, we see a dream world. When it spreads out full, this waking world of nescience comes to be." (Guru Vachaka Kovai Saying 556)

"If dream is but a whirl of thoughts, so too is waking life. The dream experience, while it lasts, is as real as what we take as real when awake." (Guru Vachaka Kovai Saying 559)

"Only so long as 'I' exists - an 'I' that sleeps, dreams and wakes - do these various states appear. When, by self-enquiry, this created ego ends, then with it ends all difference between states of Being." (Guru Vachaka Kovai Saying 568)

"The pure Self is simple Being. It does not become the objective body consciousness of the waking state. This wakeful consciousness is an associated form of consciousness involving and depending on the brain, senses and physical body. It is this

'associated consciousness' that asserts unconsciousness in the sleep state since it was not present then - when simple Being as Pure Consciousness prevailed." (Talks Number 280)

"Consciousness is our true nature. We cannot remain unconscious. We say we were unconscious in sleep since we refer to the qualified consciousness of the waking state. This relative consciousness is taken to be our self. Being absent in sleep, it asserts unconsciousness of this state. But nobody says he was unconscious while he is actually in the sleep state." (Talks Number 306)

"Not only when a world is present (in waking and dream), but also when no world is present (as in sleep), you shine as the bodiless Being. This is your true nature as the Self." (Guru Vachaka Kovai Saying 1034)

"The Self - Pure Consciousness - lies beyond the mind. When the latter rises up from the Self (in waking and dream), the world is seen and when it sets the world disappears. But the Self - the true 'I' - exists always, not rising nor setting." (Talks Number 76)

"Gods such as Ishvara and Vishnu are as real as our bodies are real. Like all our perceptions, they are all in the mind and therefore real to the mind that perceives them. Visions of God are illusory. They are only visions of the Self, objectified as the God of one's particular faith. The 'seer' - the Self - alone is real and eternal." (Talks Numbers 30, 621)

"The perceived existence and awareness of the world coincide with the rise of the mind. So both are part of the (intermittent) existence of mind and its awareness. The substratum of the mind is the Self, which is self-existent and eternally aware." (Talks Number 381)

"Anything that is seen cannot be real. The form of the Supreme is according to the desires of the seer. Thus, in the Bhagavad

Gita, Lord Krishna says to Arjuna ' See in me whatever you desire to see'." (Talks Number 364)

"Real waking - awareness of reality - lies beyond the plane of differences and therefore beyond the states of waking or dream. All perceived differences are thoughts. Thought thus obscures the reality." (Talks Number 476)

The World as Illusion

According to Advaita Vedanta, the perceived world is created by the mind under the influence of 'avidya'. Our ascribing reality to this world is considered to be in the nature of illusion, referred to as 'maya'. We do not see things as they really are. When the oneness of the totality of things is not cognized, there is particularization and this is regarded as real. **All phenomena in the world are nothing but illusory manifestations of the mind, with no reality of their own. The forms we perceive in the physical world are mere projections of the mind.**

Swami Vivekananda has explained how this happens as follows. *"What we get from the so-called external world is simply a stimulus or blow. Even to be conscious of the blow, we have to react. As soon as we react, we really project a portion of our mind (consciousness) toward the blow. When we come to know of the blow, it is really our consciousness - as it has been shaped by the blow - that we come to know. Thus, suppose we represent the 'external world' by 'x', all we really know is 'x' plus the mind, and this mind element is so strong that it has covered the whole of the 'x' which has remained unknown and unknowable throughout. If there is an external world, it is always unknown and unknowable. What we know of the world is as it has been formed and fashioned by our mind".*

"The Truth or Reality is the Self Everything that is perceived requires the Self as the perceiver, but the reality of what is perceived is only of the same degree as that of the perceiver.

What is perceived cannot exist without a perceiver - the Self - and therefore is not different from the Self. Subject and object thus merge in the Self - so in the Self or Reality, there is no seer nor objects seen, as the seer and seen are the one Self." (Talks Number 145)

"Whatever state we are in, perceptions partake of that state. In the waking state, the gross body perceives gross forms. In the dream state, the subtle body perceives subtle forms. In the state of deep sleep, - identification with a body being lost - there are no perceptions of forms. In the transcendental state, identity with Brahman places man in harmony with nature viz. oneness with all. There is nothing apart from the Self." (Talks. Number 2)

"Outlook differs with the sight of the person. Seeing with the gross eye, you perceive the gross forms. Seeing with the subtle eye (mind), you perceive the subtle. If the eye becomes the Self, which is infinite, the vision is infinite. Then there is nothing to see different from the Self." (Talks. Number 106)

"Mind is a limiting adjunct of the pure consciousness. The world is real in the same degree as the seer – the subject, object and its perception forming a triad The true reality is beyond this triad." (Talks Number 376)

"There is no use knowing all else except the Self. If the perceiver - the Self - is known, all is known. Self realization is therefore the logical and primary objective of life." (Talks 379)

"The world mocks you for knowing it without first knowing your self. The world is merely the result of your mind. Know your mind. Then see the world. You will then realize that it is not different from your Self." (Talks Number 53)

"Both the 'jnani' and the 'ajnani' perceive the world but their outlooks differ. The former is aware of the real (the Self) - the substratum, of which the world is merely a manifestation. But

the latter perceives only the manifestation and takes it to be real." (Talks. Number 65)

"Maya or illusion obscures absolute knowledge by causing it to become differentiated into the false multiplicity of the world appearance. The unity of the Absolute is fragmented." (Talks. Number 100)

"There is nothing but the Atman. The mind originates from the Atman and projects the world appearance." (Talks Number 104)

"The world is not external. The impressions cannot have an outer origin because the world can be cognized only by consciousness. The world does not assert its existence. It is merely our impression and an intermittent one at that - disappearing in the state of sleep and appearing in the wakeful state." (Talks. Number 53)

"There is only the one Consciousness which, manifesting as the 'I'-thought and identifying with the body, projects itself through the eyes and sees a world of objects outside. Being limited in the waking state, it expects to see something different from itself and the evidence of the senses is the seal of authority. In this state, one will not admit that the seer, the seen and the seeing are all manifestations of the one Consciousness – the real 'I'. In truth, there is nothing visual." (Talks. Number 196)

"Reality is that which 'is'. Everything else is only appearance and transient but we confound the appearance with the Reality that is its substratum." (Talks Number 238)

"Just as in a cinema show, a person on the screen can be seen watching a world scene, so does an illusory individual being see an illusory world in real life." (Talks. Number 443)

Not only does the ultimate conclusion of S-matrix theory viz. that the properties of sub-atomic particles can be derived from the general principles (and therefore depend on our scientific observational framework) come close to Eastern philosophical thought, but also its view of matter. It sees the world of sub-atomic particles as a dynamic network of events and emphasizes change and transformation rather than fundamental and separate structures and entities. All phenomena in this world of transformation and change are seen as dynamically related.

The Cosmic Law and Karma

Hindu metaphysics regards this dynamic network and inter-relation of events as a cosmic law - the law of karma - but is not concerned with expounding any patterns in this network or interconnectedness of events. The ego - the notion of individuality - and the concomitant sense of 'doership' are the seeds or basis of 'karma'. The kind of world we are born into, and our experiences therein, are just the return of works on the doer (the ego) - a consequence of the cosmic law of 'karma'. *The law is an intrinsic property of a supreme power - the Self - a characteristic of its very nature.* The individual organism is the working mechanism intended to produce that requital to the doer (the ego), in the form of actions and their consequences of happiness and suffering. *This process goes on until the ego - the false notion of one's individuality and doership - is dispelled. The seed of 'karma' is thus consumed and further rebirths are impossible.*

'Karma' therefore applies so long as a person imagines that he is separate from the Self and therefore the 'doer' of his actions. Once one realizes the Self however, there is no separateness and therefore no one left to experience the consequences of actions. This cosmic law then ceases to apply. It is transcended.

"If we are the agents of deeds, we shall have to experience the fruit of deeds. When one knows oneself by inquiring as to who

is the agent of deeds, the sense of agency is lost and karma is nullified. Eternal is the state of release (from karma)." (Verse 38. Forty Verses on Reality)

"If the ego upon whom 'karma' depends merges in its source - the Self - and so loses its form, how can 'karma' which depends on it survive? When there is no 'I', there is no karma." (S. Natananda - Spiritual Instruction of Bhagavan Ramana Maharshi, p.21)

"All actions take place because of the mere presence of the Self. One is troubled (i.e. subject to 'karma'), because, by identifying with the ego (the 'I' thought or individual existence), one forgets this and falsely assumes doership for actions." (Talks Number 68)

"Here, right now, is a wonder of wonders. Listen. It is the bustling, hustling zeal in action of folk who would not even be able to think at all unless they are, by omnipresent Awareness, made to think." (Guru Vachaka Kovai Saying 168)

"Assumption by the ego of the role of doer of actions is comparable to a person claiming that he moved when, in fact, only the conveyances in which he travelled moved. Just as the movement of the conveyances is confounded with his own, so also does one tend to confound what is God's activity as one's own." (Talks Number 78)

"When the Self is realized (upon dissolution of the ego) world phenomena will be regarded with indifference. One will act in the world like an actor in a drama, without attachment to the activities one engages in. All activity will nevertheless go on as ordained by the Supreme Power. The body will complete the task for which it came into being." (Talks Number 653)

"Since one is not the body, one is truly not the doer of actions. Therefore one should act without supposing that oneself is the *doer of actions. All actions will go on despite the loss of the ego sense. Each one has manifested for a particular purpose that will be fulfilled whether or not the sense of doer-ship prevails." (Talks. Number 643)*

"While for bearing the burden (of the problems of the world), there is the Lord, to imagine that the pseudo-self bears it is a mockery like the (imagined) bearing of the temple tower by the (load carrying) figures sculpted on its base. Whose fault is it if a man travelling in a cart and carrying a heavy load carries it on his head without placing it in the cart?" (Verse 17. Supplement to the Forty Verses on Reality)

"If one asks 'How can deeds get done when doership is lost? Do we not see deeds done by muktas?' The answer is 'They being egoless, it is the Supreme Himself who, dwelling in their hearts, performs these deeds.' " (Guru Vachaka Kovai Saying 1139)

"Karma Yoga is that spiritual path where a person does not arrogate to himself the role of actor. The question of renouncing the fruit of (good) actions arises only so long as there is the ego and the associated sense of doership." (Talks Number 643)

"What we experience now is only the fruit of former actions. Knowing this, one should not worry what happens to one. Whether or not one likes it, one may not escape, one must needs eat, the food one has prepared." (Guru Vachaka Kovai Saying 150)

"The spiritual aspirant must act without identifying with the body that performs the action, by abiding as his true Self. The purpose of one's birth will be fulfilled whether one wills it or not, since all actions are pre-ordained (by the law of karma)." (Talks Number 189)

"Upon surrender to the Higher Power, that Power sees your affairs through. You are no longer affected by your actions, nor by the fruits thereof, but the work goes on unhampered. Whether this Power is recognized or not, the scheme of things does not alter. Only, there is a change of outlook i.e. there is no sense of doership. Why should you bear your load on your head when you are travelling in a train?" (Talks Number 503)

"One must realize that one is not the doer of actions but is merely the instrument of a Higher Power. Then actions are not one's own (since one does not claim doership) and the fruits of actions cannot accrue to one. Until the idea of doership disappears, one has the notion of acting or refraining from action. But in reality, one is being 'manipulated' by the Higher Power (obliged to act in a particular way due to the automatic operation of the law of karma). Therefore it is best to be fixed in the Self and act without any sense of doership." (Talks Number 58)

"Just as women carrying water pots on their heads chat with their companions while balancing the pots carefully, so does the enlightened one engage in worldly activities; but they do not disturb him since his mind rests in Brahman." (Talks Number 231)

"The answer to the question as to how work can be done satisfactorily without concentrating the mind on the work is this. The mind promoting the work is merely a projection of the Self that appears in the waking state. All activity is due to the mere presence of the Self but the mind falsely assumes doership and responsibility when it rises." (Talks Number 76)

"If you remember who you really are viz. the Self, your work will not bind you. It will proceed automatically. Effort is the bondage. Make no effort either to work or to renounce work. What is ordained to happen will happen." (Talks Number 268)

"Upon realization, the Self is experienced as the sole reality, and actions are merely phenomena that do not affect the Self. When the sage (or enlightened person) acts, he has no sense of being the doer. Actions are involuntary and he merely remains a witness to them, without motive or attachment. The spiritual aspirant must practice such an attitude to work. Then it will gradually cease to hinder meditation." (Talks Number 17)

The Essence of Quantum Reality

As all phenomena are dynamically inter-related, it is considered a false attitude to think in terms of things rather than of processes in the stream of change.

"These 'things' are merely sections in the stream of change. We regard as permanent and real the products of an incessant series of transformations whereas the reality is continuous movement or change." [29]

In both Eastern thought and S-matrix theory, the emphasis is on processes rather than objects In S-matrix theory, these processes are the particle interactions that give rise to all the phenomena in the world of hadrons. In Eastern thought, the basic processes, called 'changes', are regarded not as fundamental laws imposed on the physical world but rather as the result of an innate tendency that causes them to take place naturally and spontaneously. The same too can be said of the interactions in the particle world of physics. They also reflect the innate tendencies of the particles, which are expressed in S-matrix theory in terms of reaction probabilities.

Modern physics has thus come to see the 'things' of the sub-atomic world as in Eastern thought. Stress is laid upon change and transformation, and particles are regarded as transient stages in an ongoing cosmic process. It has come to share with Eastern mysticism the view that the constituents of matter and the basic phenomena involving

them are all interconnected. They cannot be understood as isolated entities but only as integrated parts of a unified whole.

In quantum theory, the basic quantum inter-connectedness between spatially separated events is based on signals - called local connections - that are in the nature of particles or networks of particles. They cannot therefore travel faster than the speed of light. *More recent research in subatomic physics has however indicated that events in the universe appear to be interconnected in even subtler ways - by connections that are instantaneous.* These - called non-local connections - are now being seen as the very essence of the quantum reality, where individual events do not always have a well-defined cause and only their probability can be predicted. It is because these instantaneous connections are unpredictable that the laws of atomic physics are statistical laws - according to which the probabilities for atomic events are determined by the dynamics of the whole system. Thus, whereas in classical physics the properties and behaviour of the parts were considered to determine those of the whole, in quantum physics it is the whole that determines the behaviour of the parts.

In the macroscopic world of everyday experience one is able to speak of separate objects and formulate laws governing their behaviour in terms of certainties, because the instantaneous connections are relatively unimportant. But at the more fundamental and smaller dimensions, these instantaneous connections become stronger; certainties give way to probabilities; and it is increasingly difficult to separate parts from the whole.

Einstein could not accept the fundamental role of probability dictated by the existence of instantaneous connections. He believed that reality consisted of independent, spatially separated events and that events were causally and precisely determined by the signals viz. particle exchanges, of quantum theory. This position was however demolished by the famous

EPR experiment (so called after its formulators Einstein, Podolsky and Rosen) and by the theorem of John Bell. Both these proved that *the concept of reality as consisting of separate parts joined by local connections is incompatible with quantum theory.*

The EPR experiment showed that when one member of an electron pair with a total spin of zero was given an axis of rotation arbitrarily, the other member of the pair also *instantaneously* acquired a spin along the chosen axis. There was no time for it to receive that information by a conventional signal (which cannot travel faster than the speed of light). Since the signal was instantaneous, the two electrons - though far apart in space - must therefore be regarded as forming an indivisible whole linked by instantaneous connections that transcend the usual notions of information transfer. The experiment thus provided a clear demonstration that *the universe is a fundamentally interconnected, interdependent and inseparable whole and not composed of independent and spatially separated entities.*

Ramana Maharshi also emphasized the unity and undifferentiated nature of Reality.

"Unity is the reality. The perceived variety of forms is false and obstructs knowledge of the unity of Reality." (Talks Number 354)

"The differences in the world appearance are superficial. A unity runs through the diversity. It is the Self Perception of this unity is true knowledge that dispels the problems that arise from taking the diversity for real." (Talks Number 507)

"All other kinds of knowledge are trivial. The only true and perfect knowledge is the stillness of pure awareness. The many differences perceived in the Self, whose nature is awareness are wrong attributions and not real at all." (Guru Vachaka Kovai. Saying 422)

"It is a unity that the 'jnani' perceives in all differences. He is aware of distinctions but knows that they are very superficial; not substantial or permanent. What is essential in all the appearances is the one truth, the real. He perceives the one reality in all of them. Whether he moves, talks or acts, it is all the one reality in which he moves, talks or acts. There is nothing for him but the one supreme reality." (Sat-Darshana Bhashya pp. 30-31)

"The 'I' is false; 'this world' is false; the seeing of 'this world' by 'I' is false. The primal ignorance of maya that creates the triad is also false. The sole reality is the bright, marvellous inner space, Being-Awareness." (Guru Vachaka Kovai. Saying 1017)

The S-matrix theory and the bootstrap approach - both of which do not accept any fundamental, independent and separate entities but try to understand nature entirely through its self-consistency - represent the culmination of current scientific thinking. Many physicists however still do not accept this theory as it is too foreign to their traditional way of thinking, but the most outstanding physicists of the present time do not fall into this category.

As indicated earlier, *the bootstrap theory of particles has been able to account for the observed quark structure without any need to concede the existence of physical quarks.* In the conventional quark model, particles are pictured as billiard balls containing smaller billiard balls. But according to S-matrix theory, which is holistic and dynamic, particles are inter-related energy patterns in an ongoing universal process - the cosmic dance of energy. *The quark structure i.e. hadrons seeming to consist of physical quarks, merely reflects the fact that the transfer of energy and flow of information in the inseparable interconnected universe takes place along ordered and well-defined lines, resulting in well-defined patterns.* The statement *that hadrons consist of quarks is thus explained in dynamic terms.*

Order in the Universe

A key element in the bootstrap theory is the notion of order in the inter-connectedness of subatomic processes. The quark structure of hadrons is a manifestation of order and a necessary consequence of self-consistency. The need to postulate quarks as physical constituents of hadrons is obviated. The quark patterns are the only ordered relationships compatible with the properties of the S-matrix.

It is significant that the notion of order, like the principles on which the S-matrix is based, plays a very basic role in scientific methods of observation and the scientific approach to reality. **The ability to recognize order - usually in the form of patterns - seems to be an essential feature of the rational mind.** Patterns of matter and patterns of mind are increasingly being recognized as reflections of each other. Mystics have however long been aware of the intimate connection between matter (the world) and mind.

"It is possible to visualize the world as imagination or thought if the mind that comprehends the physical space is itself conceived as space. The mind space is contained in transcendental space (the Self or Pure Consciousness) and itself contains the physical space. Thoughts appearing in mind space result in physical objects in physical space i.e. the world appearance." (Talks Number 451)

"The mind is like 'akasa' (space ether). Just as there are objects in physical space, there are thoughts (as objects) in mind space. Physical space is the counterpart of mind space and the objects in physical space are the counterparts of thoughts in mind space. One cannot therefore hope to arrive at the truth behind worldly objects and phenomena because they

are mental creations. It is like trying to stamp on the head of one's shadow with one's foot. The further one moves, the further the shadow moves too. As the universe is merely a creation of the mind, it has its being in the mind. One must therefore reach the source of the mind - the Self - to reach the universe." (Talks Number 485)

"Just at the moment of rising up, the mind is only pure awareness - mind ether. Subsequently, the thought 'I am this' rises up, and this 'I' thought gives rise to other thoughts that form the individual 'jiva' and the world These are modes of the mind manifested as (physical) objects in the space ether. Again, just as the physical ether, though accommodating the gross objects, is itself the content of the mind ether, so also the latter is itself the content of the Chit (Pure Knowledge) ether." (Talks. Number 589)

S-matrix theory is also now moving towards including consciousness explicitly in future theories of matter, and studying the relation between consciousness and matter. The most advanced work in this field has been by the distinguished physicist David Bohm. Starting with the notion of 'unbroken wholeness', Bohm regards the local instantaneous connections revealed by the EPR experiment both as a crucial aspect of the wholeness of the cosmos, and as the source of the probabilistic formulation of the laws of quantum physics. He has gone beyond probability to explain - at a deeper non-manifest level - the order that he believes to be inherent in the cosmic web of relations. At this level, the interconnections of the whole have nothing to do with locality in space and time but exhibit an entirely new property viz. that of enfoldment. The term means that each part, in some sense, contains the whole. *Bohm's view is that an 'implicate order' based on this property of enfoldment prevails at the un-manifest level, and that the universe is structured on this principle.*

Bohm expresses this essential dynamic nature of reality at the subatomic level by the term 'holomovement'. It is a dynamic phenomenon out of which all forms of the material world flow. Space and time also emerge as forms flowing out of holomovement and are therefore enfolded in its order.

To understand the implicate order, Bohm has found it necessary to include consciousness as an essential feature of the holomovement and take it into account explicitly in his theory. **Mind and matter are seen as being inter-dependent and correlated but not causally connected. They are mutually enfolding projections of a higher reality - a First Cause - whose design is served by the observed behaviour of subatomic particles. In other words, the goal or design of the First Cause is the reason for the observed particle behaviour.**

Bohm's theory of an implicate order and Chew's bootstrap theory are both based on a similar view of the world as a dynamic web of relations. Both assign a central role to the notion of order. They also recognize that consciousness may be an essential aspect of the universe that will have to be eventually included in any future complete theory of physical phenomena. Such a theory may well emerge from the merging of the two theories which today represent the most philosophically profound scientific approaches to the ultimate reality.

CHAPTER 7

A SELF-CONSISTENT UNIVERSE

The idea of basic building blocks has been shown to be untenable by modern physics Historically, atoms, atomic nuclei, and then hadrons have been, in turn, considered to be the elementary particles constituting matter. But each time, these particles have been shown to be of a composite nature. Atomic, and later subatomic, physics have instead revealed a basic interconnectedness of matter - showing first that the energy of motion can be transferred into mass; and later, that particles are processes rather than objects or physical substance. These developments have strongly indicated that the simple mechanistic picture of basic building blocks must be abandoned, but many physicists are still reluctant to do so.

The Bootstrap Theory

Modern physics has led to the view that nature cannot be reduced to fundamental entities such as elementary particles or fundamental fields. **Nature has to be understood through its self-consistency.** *This is the essence of the 'bootstrap theory' which is presently being developed both as a specific theory of particles and as a philosophy of nature.*

The bootstrap theory - which was originated by Geoffrey Chew - states explicitly that the world cannot be understood as an assemblage of fundamental entities that cannot be analyzed further. It sees the universe as a dynamic web of inter-related events. None of the properties of any part of this web is fundamental. They follow from the properties of the other

A Self-Consistent Universe 125

parts, and the overall consistency of their mutual relations determines the structure of the web. *The theory not only denies the existence of fundamental constituents of matter but also accepts no fundamental entities whatsoever - either laws or principles. It is therefore a final rejection of the mechanistic worldview by modern physics. The basic philosophy embodied in the theory is however in harmony with Eastern religious philosophies - both in its worldview and its specific picture of matter.* [31]

Like the mystics, modern physicists have now come to regard all theories of natural phenomena and 'laws of nature' as creations of the human mind. They are now seen merely as features of our conceptual map of reality and not properties of reality itself. This conceptual scheme is limited and approximate, as are all its theories and laws. Belief in fundamental laws had arisen from belief in a divine lawgiver, which is deeply rooted in the Jewish-Christian tradition.

Since all natural phenomena are ultimately interconnected, we need to understand 'all' that occurs in order to explain any one of them fully. This is clearly impossible. The attitude of science has been to progress through successive approximations. One studies and describes selected groups of phenomena to gain an approximate understanding of nature - neglecting other phenomena that are deemed less relevant Different aspects of nature are thus understood in an approximate way without having to understand everything at once.

The methodology of science is therefore to construct a sequence of partial and approximate theories - each one more accurate than its predecessor. None is claimed to be a final account of the totality of natural phenomena. The incomplete nature of a theory is reflected in its arbitrary parameters or 'fundamental constants' which are quantities whose numerical values are empirical and yet to be explained. According to the 'bootstrap' philosophy, the arbitrary parameters that are presently regarded as 'fundamental constants' of nature will be explained, one by one, in future theories of increasing scope and accuracy. The ideal situation will, in this way, be approached where the theory will no longer contain any unexplained fundamental constants, and where all its 'laws' will follow from the requirement of overall self-consistency. Even so, any scientific theory will require the acceptance, without explanation, of the concepts that form the scientific language.

The requirement of mutual self-consistency of all phenomena in the universe, which forms the basis of the bootstrap theory, and the inter-relation and 'oneness' of all phenomena - postulated by all Eastern religious philosophies - are just different aspects of the same idea. An indivisible universe where all things, beings and events are inter-related can hardly make sense unless it was self-consistent. The laws of nature are thus inherent in nature and not imposed by a divine lawgiver. It is the law to which all parts of a whole have to conform because of their very existence as parts or manifestations of an indivisible whole. The law arises from the need to fit precisely into place with the other parts of the whole that they compose.

Self-consistency is therefore the essence of all the laws of nature. This view is now held both in modern science, following the development of the bootstrap theory, and in the Eastern religious philosophies where it is expressed in the law of 'karma'. The latter asserts that human affairs and natural phenomena are all made just exactly to fit into place. Law means the exact fitting into place without the slightest excess or deficiency. **The concept of self-consistency that is central to the bootstrap theory thus provides a scientific basis for the law of 'karma', which asserts that there is a natural interconnectedness and unavoidability in all human affairs and natural phenomena.**

No single phenomenon can be fully understood in isolation because of the essential inter-relatedness and indivisibility of the whole. Scientists, as indicated earlier, are satisfied with progressively improving their understanding of Nature by the methodology of science. The mystics are however not content, or even concerned with such knowledge - which they regard as relative knowledge or lower knowledge - since they realize that there is nothing explainable. Everything is a consequence of all the rest. They are concerned with absolute knowledge or higher knowledge - the Truth. The latter is a direct, non-intellectual and plenary experience of the unity of all things and the totality of existence in all its manifestations.

The Nature of Knowledge

According to Advaita Vedanta, our empirical or relative knowledge is based on the distinction of knower, knowledge and known, whereas Reality is free from all distinctions and relationships. The Reality or Brahman is pure, indivisible, infinite and eternal Existence-Awareness. It simply 'is', and is also 'all that is'. It cannot therefore be an object of such knowledge. **All thought struggles to know the real, but it can know the real only by relating it to something else. Thought thus equates the real with something else i.e. the unreal, and attributes to the real what is different from it.** This is called 'adhyasa'. What we attribute to the real is something less than it - merely an appearance thereof. Empirical knowledge thus imposes our sensory perceptions of forms etc on the one eternal and formless Existence-Consciousness It is a negation of the reality. **All relative knowledge must, strictly speaking, be regarded as 'avidya', non-knowledge or ignorance while the ascertainment (by direct experience) of the ultimate Existence-Consciousness, by the exclusion of all that is superimposed on it, is alone 'vidya'', true knowledge and the transcending of ignorance.**

"There is no (objective) knowledge apart from (metaphysical) ignorance; and there is no ignorance apart from (that) knowledge. To whom are that knowledge and that ignorance?

The knowledge that knows thus the Self that is their ground principle is (true) knowledge." (Verse 10. Forty Verses on Reality)

"How can the knowledge of objects arising in relative existence to one that knows not the truth of himself, the knower, be true knowledge? If one rightly knows the truth of him named 'I' (the Self) in whom both knowledge and its opposite subsist, then, along with ignorance, (objective) knowledge also will cease." (Verse 11. Forty Verses on Reality)

"What is other than (objective) knowledge and ignorance - that is true knowledge. Objective knowledge cannot be true knowledge. Since the Self shines without there being anything else (for it) to know or to be known (by), it is (true) knowledge. It is not nullity." (Verse 12. Forty Verses on Reality)

"The Self who is Consciousness is alone real, and nothing else. All so-called knowledge, which is manifold, is only ignorance. This ignorance is unreal since it has no existence of its own, apart from the Self." (Verse 13. Forty Verses on Reality)

These verses express Maharshi's teaching on the topic of knowledge. True knowledge is pure, unconditioned Awareness. It is the Self - the sole Reality. Ignorance (avidya) projects a non-real world that obscures knowledge of this Reality. Objective knowledge is knowledge pertaining to the objects of this unreal world and is therefore regarded as being rooted in ignorance. Hence the statement, 'there is no knowledge without ignorance'. The word 'knowledge' here signifies this objective knowledge, which is really ignorance since it is a negation of pure knowledge.

Objective knowledge comprises transformations of the pure unconditioned Awareness, and so this Awareness is the basis of the objective knowledge that is really ignorance. Mental ignorance i.e. non-knowledge of anything also cannot exist apart from the pure unconditioned Awareness, since without basic awareness, non-knowledge of anything is not possible. One's not knowing has its basis in awareness. Hence the statement, 'there is no ignorance without knowledge' The word 'knowledge' here refers to unconditioned Awareness that is true knowledge, while the word 'ignorance' includes both types of ignorance viz. metaphysical ignorance as well as mental ignorance.

The ground principle behind both (objective) knowledge and ignorance is therefore the pure unconditioned Awareness that is the Self. In the state of pure unconditioned Awareness, there is no room for ignorance since the latter represents conditioned Awareness. Both cannot co-exist. Ignorance can therefore be removed if one strives to attain the Self i.e. the state of pure Awareness. To do so, it is first necessary to understand that objective knowledge is not knowledge at all but merely a play of ignorance; and so wisdom lies, not in accumulating objective knowledge but in discovering the true nature of the Self.

The Self or the state of pure unconditioned awareness, in which objects are known to be illusory, is not a void because, while the particular contents of awareness may be shown to be unreal, the Awareness itself cannot be denied. This pure Awareness alone qualifies to be regarded as true knowledge since knowledge - to be knowledge - must be self luminous i.e. its luminosity must not be dependent on anything else. It fulfils this condition because, while being the basis of i.e. illuminating, all objective knowledge, it cannot be known, illuminated or manifested by anything else.

So long as we do not attain to higher knowledge - which can be reached only by rising to a higher state of consciousness - our empirical or relative knowledge is valid; but it remains on the same plane as the premises on which it is based. They are not on the plane of absolute reality. **The empirical world and the empirical self are both of the same rank of reality, - standing in a causal relationship to each other.** What we, as empirical egos, find in the world, we ourselves - as transcendental subjects - have placed there! All sources of knowledge are therefore valid and have relative value for the finite understanding or intellect, but only until the ultimate truth is gained.

"He, who by questing inward for the Knower, has destroyed the ego and transcended so-called knowledge, abides as the Self. He alone is a true knower, not one who has not seen the Self and therefore has an ego still." (Guru Vachaka Kovai Saying 133)

"The knowledge that ignores the Self, the knower, and holds as true the field perceived, is but illusive folly. No matter how much one has learned, true knowledge is the merging of all objective knowledge in awareness of the Self." (Guru Vachaka Kovai Saying 420)

"All other kinds of knowledge are base, trivial. The only true and perfect knowledge is the stillness of pure awareness. The many differences perceived in the Self, whose nature is Awareness, are wrong attributions and not real at all." (Guru Vachaka Kovai Saying 422)

"There is room for knowing and not-knowing only in the ego's knowledge of objects. In Awareness pure, - our sole Being - there is neither the knowing or not-knowing of objects. This alone is knowledge true." (Guru Vachaka Kovai Saying 545)

"What if one knows the subtle secrets of manifold inscrutable mysteries? Until one knows the Awareness that reveals all other knowledge, does one know the Truth?" (Guru Vachaka Kovai Saying 424)

"Only he who fondly thinks he sees the world that falsely seems to be there – when truly the Self alone exists – only to him the flood of relative knowledge is omniscience. To the jnani

A Self-Consistent Universe

beyond illusion, all such knowledge is mere hallucination."
(Guru Vachaka Kovai Saying 928)

"The learned man who, letting go the Self - the real Being - sees and cherishes this dream (the false illusory world) may be a scholar. Something different is he who has gained the clarity of Knowing the Self; he is a Knower." (Guru Vachaka Kovai Saying 1155)

Freeing the mind from thoughts and the desire for explanations is therefore one of the aims of Eastern mysticism. So long as we seek explanations, we are trapped in a conceptual network of our own making. Liberation depends on transcending the bondage imposed by thought, which can never arrive at the vision of Reality. **When one shakes off one's sense of individuality, one is lifted up into one's universal essence - the Self or Reality - and the goal is reached. But it is no more thought. It is the state of Being-Consciousness that prevails when the individual strips himself of all finite conditioning, including his intellect. Thought expires in experience, or to put it differently, relative knowledge is lifted up into true knowledge or wisdom.**

There are three sources of knowledge viz. sensory perception, inference and scriptural testimony. The Vedas are scriptural testimony to knowledge that is not open to the senses or to thought, but which has been gained by the Hindu mystics or sages in a higher state of consciousness. While the experience has the highest degree of clarity, it is not easily or clearly describable since, in this instance, language and logic attempt to say what language and logic were not invented to say. *Just as in matters of science, we accept what scientists have discovered, we must listen in the same way to mystics in spiritual matters. The mind must not set itself as a judge of what is beyond the normal state of consciousness.*

That the truth of the ultimate Reality cannot ever be ascertained through sensory perception or inference, has been amply proved by the discoveries of modern physics. Since interpretations of the direct knowledge of Reality are fallible and subject to constant revision, the Upanishads are to be looked upon merely as interpretations of the nature of Reality or Truth. They seek to give us the highest logical approximation to the Truth, which is the oneness and sole reality of Brahman - until we ourselves can gain the direct experience.

Empirical or relative knowledge of a pluralistic universe is Truth, as seen from the standpoint of empirical consciousness and it is not absolutely untrue. The universe extended in time and space is relative to the limited vision of our intellect and not final. The higher monistic and the lower pluralistic views of the universe cannot however be true in the same sense. The latter is therefore said to be lower knowledge while the former is higher knowledge. The lower knowledge is not illusory but only relative i.e. it is not absolute knowledge. The lower knowledge eventually leads us to the higher knowledge or wisdom. **The erroneous notion of empirical existence ceases when its substratum of Brahman is realized.**

"Sense perceptions can only be indirect knowledge - not direct knowledge - as they are experienced only with the aid of the senses. Only one's own awareness of being is direct knowledge as no aids are required to know one's own self." (Talks Number 92)

"The physical world arises from where you yourself arise. So one should know oneself (which is direct knowledge) before seeking to know the world (which is indirect knowledge)." (Talks Number 199)

"Realization is of Perfection. It cannot be comprehended by the mind. One must transcend the mind to 'be' the Self, which is absolute knowledge The present (relative) knowledge - of the mind - is only of limitation. The absolute knowledge of the Self is unlimited. Being so, it cannot be comprehended by this

(relative) knowledge. Cease to be a knower; then there is Perfection." (Talks Number 147)

"All worldly knowledge and experience are based on a false 'I'. It is therefore based on a flimsy foundation. What can anyone know without first knowing the true 'I' that is the Self." (Talks Number 43)

"Realization of the Self is pure (absolute) knowledge. Relative knowledge is merely conceptual whereas the pure knowledge is direct experience It is far more subtle form of knowledge than even the subtlest relative knowledge." (Talks Number 204)

"All relative knowledge is true only from the standpoint of the individual 'knower'. Since the individual knower is limited, such knowledge will also be limited. So there will always be ignorance of what lies beyond the known." (Talks Number 278)

"Relative knowledge is due to the ego or mind and is therefore relative to the subject (ego or mind). It does not pertain to the Self or Reality. It is illusory and impermanent – appearing only in the waking state and vanishing in sleep. One should go beyond such relative knowledge and abide in the Self. The Awareness that is the nature of the Self is absolute; there is no subject-object relationship here i.e. no duality. Such experience is true knowledge, and not just what is apprehended by the mind." (Talks Number 285)

"It is the one Self that is mistakenly perceived as this vast, varied universe. True omniscience is direct experience of this non-dual Self and nothing else." (Guru Vachaka Kovai Saying 934)

"The Self or true 'I' is the fundamental basis of knowing (of all relative knowledge) and knowing which all is known." (Talks Number 362)

"Scriptural or scientific theories cannot reach finality because Brahman (the Self) is subtler than the subtlest perception of the mind. Also, conceptions are contained within the confines of the finite mind, whereas Brahman is infinite. Brahman is beyond all conceptions of the mind. One must therefore transcend the mind to know Brahman. Why look outwards and go on explaining phenomena (which are endless) when upon finding the seer, all phenomena are comprised in Him." (Talks Number 388)

"The intricate maze of philosophy of different schools is said to clarify matters and reveal to us the nature of reality. But, in fact, they create confusion where it need not exist. To be aware of anything, there must be the Self (Being-Awareness). So why not remain as the Self. What need is there to explain the non-self or wallow in our mental creations?" (Talks Number 392)

"Perception implies the existence of a seer and the seen. The seer is intimate (being our self) while the seen is alien to the seer. We do not however turn our attention to knowing the self-evident seer but expend effort on analyzing the seen. The more the mind is expanded in this way, the further it goes away from the Self. We must directly 'see' the seer and thus realize the Self." (Talks Number 427)

"Lending light (awareness) to the mind, (the Lord) shines in the mind. Other than by turning the mind within and lodging it in the Lord, how is it possible to think of the Lord (Pure Being-Awareness) with the mind?" (Verse 22. Forty Verses on Reality)

"True knowledge does not consist in knowing objects. This is relative knowledge. Absolute Knowledge, in its pristine purity, stands alone - the One, Unique, Transcendent Light of Consciousness We are not independent of this Pure Knowledge because It alone exists. Ignorance interposing in the form of thought, Pure Knowledge seems different from what it really is. It is seen as the (false) 'I' and the world." (Talks Number 589)

A Self-Consistent Universe

"The essence of mind is only awareness or consciousness. When the ego dominates, it functions as the reasoning, thinking or sensing faculty. The cosmic mind - not being limited by the ego sense - has nothing separate from itself and is therefore only aware. (It is pure awareness). This is what the Bible means the statement 'I am that I AM'." (Talks Number 188)

Interpenetration

In a universe that is an indivisible whole and where all forms are fluid and ever changing, there is no place for the concept of fundamental constituents of matter. *According to the philosophy of the bootstrap theory, no part of the universe is any more fundamental than any other; and the properties of any one part are determined by those of all the others. In this sense, every part may be said to 'contain' all the others.*

The Max Planck equation indicates that a single quantum of energy could have in it all the energy of the universe. The same proposition is found in the Upanishads.

"All that exists in the whole universe is also contained in the least microcosm. Brahman is both great and vast, and subtle and tiny at the same time." (Mundaka Upanishad)

"Since the minute and vast alike vanish beyond the mind, the Self - Awareness true and transcendent - holds in its embrace both vastness vaster than the vastest, and minuteness tinier than the tiniest atom." (Guru Vachaka Kovai Saying 498).

"All know the drop merges into the ocean. But very few know that the ocean merges into the drop." (Kabir, the Sufi mystic) in Prabuddha Bharata (Talks Number 50)

The concept of 'each in all and all in each' is inherent in the philosophy of Advaita Vedanta since it follows from its

basic doctrine viz. the unity and indivisibility of the whole. It implies perfect interfusion or mutual embodiment of all 'parts' of the manifest pluralistic universe. This is known in Mahayana Buddhism as 'interpenetration' It is essentially a dynamic inter-relation both in space and time. In the mystic experience, called 'sahaja samadhi' by Ramana Maharshi, there is direct experience of mutual embodiment; and space and time are also seen as interpenetrating. The solid lines of individuality melt away and there is no feeling of finiteness. It is a direct experience of the 'One pervading each and at the same time encompassing all in itself'. *Mystic vision thus sees the whole world in a grain of sand just as the modern physicist sees the world in a hadron.*

The experience of 'interpenetration' in the state of enlightenment (also called Self-realization) can be regarded as a mystical vision of the complete 'bootstrap' situation where all the phenomena in the universe merge in one harmonious whole. In this experience, intellect is transcended and causal explanations become redundant - being replaced by direct experiential knowledge of the mutual interdependence of all things and events in an indivisible whole. Models of the sub-atomic world based on the bootstrap theory show striking parallels to this mystic view.

"The state of realization is often called 'jagrat sushupti' i.e. wakeful sleep or sleeping wakefulness. There is the awareness of the waking state and also the stillness of sleep. It is the state of perfect (unqualified) awareness and perfect stillness combined. The stillness is reached with perfect awareness. If one is free from all thought and yet aware, one is that perfect Being." (Talks Number 609)

"Where one sees no other; hears no other; and knows no other - That is the state of Perfection, the Self, and the sole Reality. If the Self is known, the objects merge into one and the One without a second will shine. Until then, thoughts arise and objects will appear and disappear." (Talks Number 634)

A Self-Consistent Universe

"In the state of realization, Absolute Consciousness reigns supreme. It is not a state of 'sunya' (a blank). The appearance of a blank is due to the fact that what is to be witnessed and the witness merge (interpenetrate) in this state." (Talks Number 68)

According to the bootstrap hypothesis, the full S-matrix - and therefore all the properties of particles - can be determined uniquely from the general principles from which it is constructed because there is only one possible S-matrix that is in conformity with all of them. These principles represent the unquestioned framework upon which all science is based. In a scientific context, the formulation of the bootstrap idea is however limited and approximate because it neglects all but the strong interactions. It deals exclusively with the hadrons; is formulated on the basis of S-matrix theory; and its aim is to derive, and thus show that all the properties and interactions arise uniquely from the requirement of self-consistency. *The failure so far to construct a consistent partial S-matrix is readily explained on the basis that there can be only one consistent S-matrix, and that is the one describing 'all' the properties and interactions of particles. This is exactly the essence of the bootstrap hypothesis.* [32]

The interactions of subatomic particles are however so complex that it may never be possible to construct a complete self consistent S-matrix. But a set of partially successful models of smaller scope – each covering only a part of particle physics - can be constructed. Each model will contain some unexplained parameters that represent its limitations, but the unexplained parameters of one model will be explained by another. Thus more and more phenomena will be progressively covered with ever-increasing accuracy by a mosaic of interlocking models whose net number of unexplained parameters will keep declining. None of the individual models is any more fundamental than the others and, in so far as they are mutually consistent, such a combination of models is said to be 'bootstrapped'. [33]

The challenge to S-matrix theory and the bootstrap hypothesis has been to account for the quark structure that is so characteristic of the strong interactions. Recently however, several major developments in S-matrix theory have made it possible to explain the regularities in hadron structure and interactions without having to postulate the physical existence of quarks. The picture that is emerging is that hadrons 'involve' one another in the dynamic and probabilistic sense of S-matrix theory - each hadron being a potential 'bound state' for all the sets of particles that may interact to form that hadron. In a sense, 'every particle consists of all other particles'. Each hadron thus plays three roles. It is a composite structure; it can be a constituent of another hadron; and it can be exchanged between constituents and thus form part of the forces holding a structure together. No hadron is any more elementary than any other, and the binding forces are also hadrons.

Since each hadron is held together by forces associated with the exchange of hadrons in the cross channels, and each of these other hadrons is held together by forces to which the first hadron makes a contribution, *'each particle helps to generate other particles that in turn help to generate it'*. The whole set of hadrons thus generates itself in this way or 'pulls itself up by its bootstraps'. Hence the term 'bootstrap hypothesis' The extremely complex bootstrap mechanism is self-determining in the sense that there is only one way in which it can be achieved.

All hadrons are thus dynamically 'composed' of one another in a self-consistent way and, in that sense, can be said to 'contain' one another. In the Eastern religious philosophies, a similar concept is applied to the macrocosm or entire universe. To the mystic, every object in the universe is not merely itself but involves every other object and in fact 'is' everything else. **This vision of interpenetration cannot be grasped intellectually i.e. by the ordinary human mind, but can only**

A Self-Consistent Universe

be directly experienced by an enlightened mind i.e. one in the particular state of 'pure consciousness'. It is such a vision that the sages of India have experienced in the state known as 'sahaja samadhi' from well over 2500 years ago, before the beginning of particle physics Such sages are no more persons like us, living in our world of space and time. *The consciousness of a sage is not that of the ordinary mind, regulated by the senses and logic. The reality for such a mind has its own rules.*

The reality of the hadron bootstrap vision is somewhat similar since it is inconceivable in ordinary space and time. It too has its own rules viz. those of quantum theory and relativity theory. In this vision of reality, the forces holding particles together are themselves particles exchanged in the cross channels; and every particle 'contains' all other particles, while being at the same time a part of each of them! This cannot be visualized by the human mind since we have no intellectual comprehension of the four-dimensional world of space-time.

Consciousness and the Universe

S-matrix theory - which was developed specifically to describe the strong interactions - will eventually have to be extended to include concepts that are presently accepted without explanation, such as space-time and even that of human consciousness. Geoffrey Chew, the originator of the bootstrap theory has already conceded that, *carried to its logical extreme, the bootstrap theory must accept and include the existence of consciousness as a property of Nature, for self-consistency of the whole.* [34]

Such a view is a major step away from the mechanistic worldview of classical physics towards the position held by the Vedas, where consciousness occupies a central position. The basic thesis of the Vedas is that a 'Conscious, Supremely Intelligent Reality' - called Brahman - is the cause of the cosmos. According to the Vedas, Brahman - having awoken as the consciousness 'I AM' felt a desire to manifest itself, resulting in the creative forces that made the One Being evolve into the manifold universe.

In Advaita Vedanta, which is the highest expression of the philosophy of the Vedas, Brahman - the sole reality and substratum of the universe - is one and indivisible. Human beings are also therefore part of the inseparable, self-consistent whole, and their consciousness therefore implies that the whole too is conscious. Human beings are thus considered to be a living proof of the cosmic consciousness underlying the universe.

The Vedas assert that there is 'pure consciousness' as the substratum of every manifestation of life. This is called the 'Atma' to distinguish it from 'Paramatma' - the term given to Brahman or the Absolute Consciousness that is the substratum of the entire cosmos. The 'atma' is sometimes described in the scriptures as a 'particle' of the 'Paramatma', but in essence the two are identical, since Brahman is one and indivisible. Both life force ('prana') and mind ('manas') have their source in this Consciousness. The Absolute Consciousness confined to a body and energized by the life force, mind and subtle sense perceptions is termed the 'jivatma', which corresponds to the term 'soul'.

The degree of order, organization, integration and harmony observed in the universe also supports the Vedic thesis of Consciousness as the reality and substratum of the universe since order, integration and harmony imply intelligence and design - which in turn imply consciousness. This thesis stands in stark opposition to classical scientific theory, which postulated a purely mechanistic concept of the universe. The 'Big Bang' theory of science regards the universe as the result of insentient forces; but why the 'Big Bang' occurred at the start of creation is a mystery for science. Classical science

A Self-Consistent Universe

therefore does not tell us wherein precisely lies the origin of the universe.

In contrast to the scientific approach that regards the universe as an effect and tries to trace it back to its anterior cause, the spiritual or mystic approach starts from intuitive insight into the Cause and then explains the effect in the terms of the cause. To the mystic, the Cause is a fact or reality prevailing prior to anything else, whereas to the scientist this reality is to be arrived at through data (gathered through direct and indirect sense perceptions) - which are then analyzed with the help of reason.

The following statement by James Jeans, one of the most distinguished astronomers of modern times, puts the scientific approach in its proper perspective.

"Standing on our microscopic fragment of a grain of sand, man attempts to discover the nature and purpose of the vast universe that surrounds him." [35]

The superiority of the spiritual approach over the scientific has also been conceded by no less a person than the greatest scientist of the last century.

"Cosmic religious experience is the strongest and noblest mainspring of scientific research." [36]

The superiority of the spiritual approach is understandable because the intuition of the mystic (prajna) is a profound and powerful faculty that is latent in man. It stems directly from the light of cosmic consciousness and illumines his intellect. It is therefore capable of deep insight into any phenomenon on which it is directed. When intuition is activated, revelations come forth from the inner consciousness as spontaneously as the 'I am' that arises for everyone from the same source. **Intuition is a higher level of consciousness that gives access to knowledge beyond ordinary mental perception.** As

Einstein himself discovered, it gives scientists the deep insights that make them creative.

"Pure logical thinking cannot yield us any real knowledge of the empirical world All knowledge of reality starts from experience and ends with it. Propositions arrived at by purely logical means are completely empty." [37]

Science, studying the evolution of life at a physical level, postulates that life emerged from matter through a series of physicochemical processes, followed by molecular and biochemical processes. One of the most important steps is held to be the appearance of the DNA molecule in which genetic codes are programmed and transmitted – thus providing a basis for the evolution of species of increasing complexity and organization through natural selection and differential reproduction. *The Vedas too share the concept of evolution towards higher forms of life but there is an important difference.* **Whereas science visualizes evolution as progressive development in physical complexity and mental capacity, mysticism views evolution as a trend towards perfection by a gradual unfolding of the Cosmic Intelligence in all beings.** The ultimate reduction of the phenomena of life to the properties of DNA and related substances is not very convincing. *The concepts and models of the physical sciences are not adequate to explain the biological phenomena of cell differentiation, hierarchical order, the harmonized interaction of innumerable processes, and the organization and goal-directed behaviour of living organisms and systems. They leave out precisely what is specific to life processes viz. intelligent direction by an intelligent principle. Darwin - the founder of the theory of biological evolution - himself finally admitted that he felt impelled to look to a First Cause (of the nature of an intelligent mind), in view of the impossibility of conceiving the universe as the result of blind chance or necessity.*

Classical mechanistic science has held that the emergence and evolution of life out of molecules is due to chance and physicochemical factors. Such a theory however does not even begin to explain the complexity of structure and increasing levels of organization found in nature.

"When inert molecules rise to become living molecules, some kind of higher integration takes place that cannot be adequately explained in terms of physical and chemical processes." [38]

Logic also contradicts the theory of mechanistic science since an effect cannot be of a higher order than its cause. **The emergence of life cannot therefore be explained in terms of any principle more gross than life itself. It can only arise from a source that is subtler in character than life. According to the Vedas this is Pure Consciousness.**

The essence of the Vedic view is that the creation and evolution of the universe is merely the Absolute Cosmic Consciousness (Brahman) manifesting itself. Since Brahman is infinite, eternal, unchanging, indeterminate and attribute-less, it cannot be a cause of the universe. If Brahman itself changes, it ceases to be Brahman, which is immutable. Advaita Vedanta therefore postulates a 'changing Brahman' - a supreme personality called Ishvara - who combines within himself the natures of both being and becoming, to explain the appearance of the universe. He is the mediating principle between Brahman and the universe - one with Brahman and yet related to the material universe.

The Vedas thus declare that Brahman, on which all rests, becomes Ishvara - from whom proceed the origin, the substance and the diversity of the universe. By the special qualities of his nature and his great powers, Ishvara 'transforms' himself into the universe. The universe originates from, and returns to, Ishvara. *Sankara, the great exponent of Advaita Vedanta, argues for the reality of Ishvara on the ground that the universe is not inanimate but alive and animated from within. There is therefore an inherent intelligence in all matter and it is this intelligent power - Ishvara - that results in the design and organization seen in Nature. This activity and consciousness belong to the cause of the universe - Ishvara.*

According to Sankara, the consciousness and life of Ishvara throbs in all parts of the universe, unifying all, containing all. Ishvara and the universe - the cause and effect - are identical. They are not identical as forms or modifications, but in their fundamental nature, of Brahman. Ishvara and the universe are expressions, on the plane of space and time, of what already exists potentially in Brahman i.e. both Ishvara and the world of experience are Brahman, cast in the moulds of logic and sensory perception.

The discoveries of modern physics at the most fundamental level have brought the scientific view very close to that of the Vedas. The originator of the bootstrap theory, which embodies the most advanced scientific philosophy, has admitted that the theory needs to bring in consciousness as a property of nature to ensure self-consistency of the whole. The Vedas declare Brahman or the sole Reality to be of the nature of Pure Consciousness. The scientific and mystic views of the universe thus converge and it is well expressed in the following quotation.

"The universe looks more like a great thought - as always postulated by the Vedas – than a great machine, as long believed by classical physics." [39]

Ramana Maharshi, as an exponent of Advaita Vedanta at its highest philosophical level, constantly emphasized that the Reality - which he called the Self - was pure, infinite and eternal Being-Consciousness. This is reflected in the following quotations:

"There is only the Self. Pure Consciousness and the Self are the same. Being infinite and non-dual, there can be no distinction of perceiver and perceived; there is therefore nothing to be perceived, as no subject-object relationship is

possible. The world appears to the individual because of his individualized consciousness, but this consciousness is the same as the Pure Consciousness of the Self. What appears is also the Self, as there is nothing apart from the Self." (Talks Number 420)

"Supreme, Infinite Perfect Consciousness alone is. From it arises individual finite consciousness by (illusory) limitation." (Talks Number 68)

"Being-Consciousness is always there, eternal and pure. The rising consciousness (ego 'I') rises and sets i.e. is transitory. Following its rise, the world appears. When it sets, the world disappears." (Talks Number 53)

"Cosmic Consciousness - the light of awareness - is projected from the Self (Brahman), which is Absolute Consciousness. Just as all the pictures thrown on a screen are visible by the light in which they are projected, so also all the objects and bodies forming the (perceived) universe are visible in the light of cosmic consciousness." (Talks Number 177)

"Body-consciousness springs from 'I' consciousness (the sense of individual being), which in turn rises from (Pure) Consciousness. But, in reality, this Pure Consciousness alone exists. All else are superimpositions." (Talks Number 340)

"The images seen in a mirror are analogous to the display of the cosmos on Pure Consciousness. Just as the images in the mirror cannot exist without the latter, so also the world can have no existence apart from Pure Consciousness." (Talks Number 288)

"Our existence, which we cannot deny, is the Self. The Self is Pure Consciousness. To consciously experience this viz. that we are always the ever-present Self, is realization." (Talks Number 625)

Science has attempted to trace developments at a purely physical level while mysticism has done so in terms of the underlying reality of a Cosmic Consciousness. Evolution of living beings is regarded by Vedanta as a progression from lower to higher forms of consciousness. The lowest forms have a dormant consciousness. These give way to forms with increasing alertness and dynamism and finally to forms where consciousness is highly developed, - manifesting as a sense of humanity, and intellectual ability. Evolution in this scheme has an aim viz. consciousness evolving from a state near dormancy to reach its source and fulfilment - the Cosmic Consciousness. *This Cosmic Consciousness itself has been guiding the course of this evolution from the beginning.* **Thus, according to Vedanta, the Cosmic Will of Brahman is the starting point of creation and carries with it the whole plan of creation. All manifestations of energy, matter and living forms are only the unfolding of that cosmic design.**

Following the revelations of sub-atomic research, science too is now coming round to the view that the explicit inclusion of consciousness must necessarily be an essential part of future theories of matter and the universe. After all, observations of atomic phenomena have already shown that these can be understood only as links in a chain of processes - the end of the chain lying in the consciousness of the observer. Such a future step would be immensely more profound than anything comprising the hadron 'bootstrap' We would have to confront the elusive concept of observation and also that of consciousness. It will be a completely new form of human endeavour and one that will not only lie outside physics but also not even be describable as scientific. [40]

Such explicit inclusion of consciousness in future enlargement of the bootstrap theory offers excellent prospects for direct interaction between physics and Eastern mysticism, since the understanding of one's consciousness and its relation to the perceived universe is the starting point of the mystical search for reality. If scientists wish to include consciousness in their research, a study of Eastern ideas of consciousness would therefore be a valuable source for significant new insights.

The assertions of mystics into the nature of consciousness, based on their direct mystical insights, have recently received support from scientific studies involving the use of psychedelic drugs for psychological exploration. These drugs have been found to be powerful catalysts of mental processes, thereby facilitating the emergence of unconscious materials from different levels of the mind. Their role in the exploration of the human mind has been described as being equivalent to the role played by the microscope for medical research or the telescope for astronomy. [41]

According to Grof's studies, *the unconscious mind comprises three major levels or domains.* The most superficial level is the domain of 'psychodynamic' experiences, which involves re-living of emotionally relevant memories from the past. The next level is the domain of 'perinatal' experiences, which involves extremely realistic and authentic re-living of the sensations and feelings associated with various stages of one's actual birth process. *The deepest level is the domain of 'transpersonal' experiences. It is this domain that provides deep insights into the nature and relevance of the spiritual dimension of consciousness. The experiences in this domain involve an expansion of consciousness beyond individual boundaries and thus provide an important link to Eastern approaches to consciousness.* Perceptions of the environment also transcend the usual limits of sensory perception, often approaching the direct mystical experience of the sages. As these experiences defy logical reasoning or analysis, they are almost impossible to express in factual language.

Psychedelic experiences at the perinatal level have been found to lead to the feeling that life is constant change; that the totality of one's perceptions is some fundamental illusion; and that all one's present life strategies and goals are erroneous. In their new worldview, worldly ambitions and the desire for power or material possessions fade away and the spiritual dimension of one's existence is realized to be more important, if not fundamental. The sense of separateness is lost and the world is seen in terms of energy patterns rather than of solid matter. But there is still an objective, absolute space in which everything happens and there is also linear time.

This however changes in a profound way in psychedelic experiences at the next level, the transpersonal domain. *There, the image of three-dimensional space and linear time is shattered completely. One realizes that there are alternatives not only to conceptual thinking about the world, but also to actual experience of the world.* One can experience one space intruding upon another; even simultaneous experience of spaces from different periods of time; or different modes of time such as circular or backward running time. There are other ways of experiencing things other than in a causal way.

In psychedelic sessions at the transpersonal level, there is a fundamental shift in perception. Consciousness is seen as something primordial that cannot be explained on the basis of anything else. It is something that is just there, manifest in all things and beings, and ultimately the sole reality. The questions are therefore not those of Western science viz. when consciousness originates and when matter becomes conscious of itself, but how consciousness produces the illusion of matter! The transpersonal domain is pure consciousness, indicating that one's deepest being is consciousness. This is precisely what the mystics have experienced and declared for over five thousand years.

In contrast to the Western view that matter is primary and that consciousness is a property of complex material patterns, they have always maintained that pure consciousness is the primary reality, the essence and ground of the universe and all beings - these being manifestations of that pure consciousness.

A Self-Consistent Universe

When people were in these special states of consciousness, their experience was always ineffable, beyond description, and there was a feeling of 'having arrived'. They felt intuitively that all questions had been answered. There was no need to ask any question, nor anything to be explained. In these states there is access, through visions or experience, to knowledge that is inaccessible in the ordinary state of consciousness. But this knowledge can be communicated in scientific language only if one has the prior scientific background to make the connection. Very few mystics have this background, and in any case they are not interested in objective knowledge pertaining to the material world. The potential is however there, as models of cosmology based on mystic visions have been found to be closely similar to those that subsequently emerged from astrophysics The greatest scientists have also made their most astounding discoveries about nature from insights gained during such non-ordinary states of consciousness.

Experiences from the use of psychedelic drugs have also shown that there is a continuous 'progression' in 'levels' of consciousness from that of inorganic matter, through that of plant and animal, to human consciousness. The consciousness of inorganic objects or plants is however experienced as a participatory consciousness i.e. as part of a larger mindful and conscious system - the universe - in which it participates. The mystic also experiences the consciousness inherent in everything around him in the same way i.e. as one with his universal consciousness. All things and beings are one in this cosmic consciousness.

Human consciousness is capable of two complementary modes of awareness viz. the Cartesian-Newtonian mode and the transpersonal mode. In the former, the world is perceived in terms of separate objects, three dimensional space and linear time. In the latter, the usual limitations of sensory perception are transcended and perception shifts from solid objects in space to fluid energy patterns. The first corresponds to a 'particle-like' mode of perception while the latter to a 'wave-like' mode of perception. They are therefore analogous to the particle and wave aspects of sub-atomic matter.

To perceive reality exclusively in the transpersonal mode is incompatible with functioning in the everyday world To function exclusively in the Cartesian mode is also madness. It is the madness of the present Western culture. The symptoms (not recognized as such) are an ego-centred, highly competitive and goal oriented life; inability to be genuinely satisfied with any level of wealth, power or fame; and a sense of meaninglessness and futility. It must be tempered with perception in the transpersonal mode, which confers awareness of the oneness of all life; awareness of the interdependence of all that exists; and a sense of oneness with the whole universe.

Mind and Consciousness

Recent research on the relationship between mind and consciousness has been described by Bateson, distinguished philosopher-scientist and author of *Mind and Nature* and *Steps to an Ecology of Mind*. According to Bateson, *mind is a systems phenomenon characteristic of any system that can process information and thereby exhibit the characteristics that we normally associate with mind - such as thinking, learning, memory etc. Mind is seen as a necessary and inevitable consequence when structural complexity exceeds a certain level, and precedes the appearance of any nervous system.* **Mind is immanent not only within the body, but also in information pathways outside the body. Individual human minds are thus embedded in the larger minds of ecological systems, which are, in turn, integrated into the planetary mental system - the mind of Gaia This, in turn, participates in the cosmic mind.** *There are thus larger manifestations of mind, of which our individual minds are only sub-systems. Mind exists not only in individual organisms but also in ecosystems and the universe.*

More recently, research under the leadership of Ilya Prigogine, Nobel Prize winning scientist, has resulted in the theory of self-organizing systems. According to this theory, the patterns of organization characteristic of living systems are based on the dynamic principle of 'self organization' i.e. order in the system is established by the system itself and not imposed from outside. As the criteria for self-organizing systems are almost identical to Bateson's criteria for the existence of mind, *the principles of self-organization in living systems are essentially mental.* **Mind is thus immanent in matter at all levels where it exhibits life. Mind is the essence of being alive. Mind and self-organization are a unity - merely different aspects of the same phenomenon, that of life.**

Modern systems theory sees all living organisms as self-organizing systems and different biological forms (structures) as the manifestations of underlying processes of self-organization. *Mind is the dynamics of self-organization in living systems. Awareness is a property of mind at all levels of living system complexity, since in its absence the processes bringing about self-organization would not be possible.* Capra distinguishes between mind and consciousness - defining the former as awareness and the latter as 'self-awareness'. Consciousness, in this sense, is seen as a feature of mind that appears only at its higher levels, - unfolding to its fullest extent in the human mind.

The classical Western scientific view has been that matter is primary, and that consciousness is a property of complex material patterns - emerging at a certain level of biological evolution. In contrast to this, the mystical view regards consciousness as the primary and sole reality, the essence and ground of all forms of matter and all living beings - all of which are seen as its manifestations. According to Capra, *the new systems view of mind provides an ideal framework for unifying the two views. The systems view agrees with the scientific view that consciousness is a manifestation of complex material patterns i.e. living systems of higher complexity. On the other hand, it sees the biological structures of these systems as expressions of processes that represent the system's self-organization, and hence as manifestations of mind. Material structures can therefore no longer be regarded as the primary reality. If the systems view is extended to the universe as a whole, all its structures - ranging from sub-atomic particles, organisms to galaxies - are seen as manifestations of the universe's self organizing dynamics, and therefore of a universal or cosmic mind. And this, as we have seen, is the essence of the mystic view.*

"God is not the creator, but the mind of the universe." [42]

CHAPTER 8

THE NEW ORDER

The Eastern religious philosophies are concerned with timeless mystical knowledge that lies beyond reasoning and cannot be expressed in words. *The principal theories and models of modern physics have now led to a worldview that is internally consistent and in harmony with the philosophy of Eastern mysticism.*

The Convergence of Science and Spirituality

The various approaches followed by man to understand, in a rational way, the mystery of life and the universe have resulted in various beliefs and descriptions regarding them. These emphasize different aspects, and all are valid and useful in the context in which they arose. But they are all only representations of reality and therefore limited. None gives a complete or ultimate picture of reality. Thus the mechanistic worldview of classical physics is of undoubted value in describing the physical phenomena of everyday life and for dealing with life in our physical environment. It has however proved inadequate for description of physical phenomena in the atomic and subatomic worlds.

As against this mechanistic view, there has been the view of the mystics who regard all phenomena in the universe as manifestations of a single inseparable whole. This worldview and its concepts - derived from non-ordinary experience in a non-ordinary state of consciousness - deal primarily with the nature of reality rather than the phenomena comprising the world appearance.

The vision of the ultimate reality, according to both modern science and Eastern spirituality, is today almost identical. The Vedic concept of Reality is that it is infinite, eternal, Existence-Awareness (Brahman), of which the universe is a manifestation or projection. Science has come very close to this position. Quantum theory implies that matter, in its essence, is dynamic energy that shows intelligence in its workings. At its most fundamental level, matter appears to possess 'information' and act accordingly. Similarly, relativity theory implies that consciousness is the essence of the universe since the observer and the phenomena he studies are both bound together in the same consciousness. The quantitative character of the physical world depends on the state of the observer and his frame of reference. *The protagonists of the 'bootstrap theory' have now recognized that human consciousness must be explicitly included in future theories of matter.*

Both the mechanistic view and the mystical view have a place in our daily life - the former for science and for dealing with technological problems, and the latter for a balanced and harmonious approach to life. *Beyond the dimensions of our everyday sensory environment, mechanistic concepts lose their validity and science has had to replace them with holistic concepts very similar to those used by the mystics.* **Thus modern science has found that the concepts embodied in the Eastern religious philosophies, although of little value for science and technology in ordinary life, are extremely useful in understanding phenomena at the atomic and subatomic levels. The concepts of the mystics are clearly more fundamental than those of classical physics.**

The reason for the close parallels between the worldviews of modern physicists and the mystics is not hard to discern. Both emerge when one enquires into the essential nature of things i.e. into the deeper realms of matter in physics, and into the deeper realms of consciousness in mysticism. In either case, one discovers that *reality is quite different from the superficial appearance of the everyday world. Recent advances in physics have thus exploded the myth of incompatibility between the objective knowledge associated with science and the so-called subjective knowledge associated with spirituality.*

The parallels between the views of modern physicists and mystics are due also to other factors that they share in common. Both in physics and mysticism, the methods are thoroughly empirical. Physicists derive their knowledge from experiments while mystics do so from meditative insights. But both are observations and in both cases are regarded as the sole source of knowledge. The object of observation is however totally different. *The physicist looks at a physical world that is outside himself, and which depends on his body consciousness, whereas the mystic looks within and explores his consciousness at its various levels - the lowest of which is body consciousness.* In the state of enlightenment or true knowledge the mystic directly experiences his true being or self as one with the eternal and infinite Existence-Consciousness that is the sole reality and ground of the entire universe in all its manifestations. He gains an intuitive awareness or vision of the wholeness and indivisibility of the cosmos, including himself.

"Understanding one's own truth in the truth of the omnipresent, nameless and formless Reality and being one with it - having been resolved into it - is true seeing." (Verse 8. Forty Verses on Reality)

Expressed in another way, **when one gains an insight into the reality of one's 'being', the same reality is cognized as the truth of all phenomena.**

As succinctly stated by Advaita Vedanta:

"To experience the Light of the Spirit, one has to be that Spirit oneself."

The acts of observation, both in the realm of science and mysticism, require training. In the case of science the observations are based on carefully planned experiments, while training is in developing the intellect or rational side of consciousness; in the use of sophisticated technology; and on teamwork. The resulting knowledge comprises models and theories that are approximations to reality. In the mystical approach to reality, observation is by individual meditation, and the training involves developing the intuitive side of consciousness by rigorous practice called 'sadhana'. The resulting knowledge is a holistic insight or vision into the nature of reality - a plenary and intuitive experience of its undifferentiated unity. The intellect is used merely to interpret the experience.

In the scientific approach, the approximations to reality are based on intellectual activity during the ordinary state of consciousness i.e. its tendency to measure, classify, abstract and conceptualize. Acts of observation are of phenomena in nature and in experiments. The mind is outwardly directed and guided by sensory perceptions. In mysticism, however, the act of observation comprises watching the mind. Consciousness is divorced from sensory perceptions and inwardly directed. Reality is eventually experienced intuitively 'as it is', on attaining a 'non-ordinary' state of consciousness.

Unlike the mystic, the physicist commences his enquiry into the essential nature of things by looking outwards and studying the material world. Penetrating into ever-deeper levels, he has become aware of the essential unity of all things and events, and also that he himself and his consciousness are an essential part of this unity. **Thus both the mystic and the physicist arrive at the same conclusion - one starting from the inner realm of consciousness and the other from the outer realm of the physical world. In this harmony of views, science confirms the ancient Vedic wisdom - that Brahman, the ultimate reality without, is identical with the 'Atma', the reality within.**

"The (objects of the) physical world arises from where you yourself arise. (Their substratum is therefore the same viz. Absolute Consciousness). The apparent difference between yourself and the world is only with reference to the body and arises with body awareness. If you turn your vision inwards, the whole world will be full of the Supreme Spirit. Even the material sciences trace the origin of the universe to some one primordial matter - exceedingly subtle." (Talks Number 199)

"The One, which alone exists, is the Reality. It is the Existence-Awareness that appears as the world, the things we see and we ourselves." (Talks Number 186)

"The world is, in reality, spiritual alone (pure Being-Consciousness). Because we identify with our physical bodies, the world also appears to be physical i.e. material substance. But 'That' which exists is spiritual alone; and it will be realized to be so, if one realizes that one's true nature is infinite spirit alone. Then one is free from the limitations that the gross or subtle bodies impose." (Talks Number 328)

"The 'jnani', like the 'ajnani', has the 'I am the body' notion. But whereas the 'ajnani' thinks that only his own body is 'I', the 'jnani' knows that all (the entire cosmos) is his body since the Self 'Brahman' is infinite." (Talks. Number 383)

A further similarity between the ways of the physicist and the mystic is the fact that their observations relate to realms inaccessible to the ordinary senses - the subatomic world in the case of the physicist, and non-ordinary states of consciousness in tne case of the mystic. In both cases, a multi-dimensional experience transcends the sensory world and is impossible to express in ordinary language. **Science has thus been obliged to give up its premise that the intellect can arrive at the reality and express it in words and concepts. The premise of mysticism viz. that the absolute reality transcends the**

intellect and is indescribable, since it is beyond the realm of the senses and intellect, stands vindicated.

The mystic and the modern physicist therefore have much in common and the parallels in their view of the world are consequently not too surprising. *Science and mysticism seem to be two complementary manifestations of the human mind - of its rational and intuitive faculties. The scientist experiences the world through an extreme specialization of the rational mind. The mystic does so by extreme specialization of the intuitive mind. Neither is encompassed in the other nor reducible to the other, but both are necessary - supplementing each other for gaining a fuller understanding of reality and the world.* In science, knowledge is based on experiment but must be complemented by intuition to provide insights. In mysticism, on the other hand, knowledge is based on mystical insight but the intellect has to be used to interpret the experience.

It may be said that science is born of man's inbuilt craving for intellectual understanding of the world around him, while spirituality arises from even deeper within his being. It is the yearning of his individual consciousness to shed its limitations and merge into the Pure Infinite Eternal Consciousness that is its source. **Science thus leads to truth at one level whereas spirituality leads to truth at a deeper level.**

The intuitional experience of Reality has the highest degree of clarity but it is not easily conceptualized. In trying to interpret and express through language the intuitive experience of reality, we are attempting to say what language and logic were not invented to say.

Science, Spirituality and Worldly Life

Science, in its practical sense, does not need mysticism nor does mysticism need science but mankind needs both. The mystic viewpoint and experience is needed to possess an understanding and vision of the deepest nature of phenomena and events, while science is needed for practical life in the everyday world. What is required therefore is not a synthesis but a dynamic interplay between mystical intuition and a scientific approach towards worldly living. Science and spirituality are like two legs and a man needs both to live happily in harmony with the world, and at the same time progress towards self-fulfilment. Without science, life can be a hard struggle, but without spirituality he is little more than an aggressive animal. *Scientific knowledge enables man to live in the world free from want and hardship. But the vision of mysticism is necessary in order to reveal to him his true nature and that of the world. It enables him to know his true purpose in life and how life should be lived in consonance with this overall purpose. Conviction in the divinity of one's real nature also gives one the spiritual strength to face the struggles of life with equanimity.*

"I have never, over a career of over sixty years, come across a single person with spiritual strength who needed the attention of a psychiatrist." [43]

During the last century in particular, the progress of science has fostered a materialistic outlook on life that tended to dehumanize those sections of mankind that have based their approach to life on science alone. The higher values in life that were long cherished have succumbed to the forces of greed, selfishness and competition ushered in by the new philosophy of unadulterated materialism. Progress in science and technology has given man such awesome powers that his value perceptions and aims in life have been almost completely degraded. The conflicts and social problems that beset the world today are the result. As mentioned earlier, the vision provided by mysticism must be sought to provide guidance as to man's true purpose in life and how it should be lived.

"Only a true religion and spirituality based thereon can save mankind from walking towards self destruction." [44]

The Eastern religious philosophies have provided us both a worldview based on direct mystic experience of Reality, as well as the principles on which worldly action should be based. One of the best known of Indian works in this context is the highly revered Bhagavad Gita In more recent times, the sage Ramana Maharshi (1889-1950) devoted his life to propagating a spiritual philosophy and a practical approach to living that are more suited to the modern age. It involves the spiritual practice of 'Self enquiry' to realize the true nature of oneself and the world, combined with worldly action in consonance with the true nature of Reality. One is 'in the world but not of it' i.e. one follows the inner spiritual quest but conforms to the outward conditions of life, anchored in the intellectual conviction that both one's body and the world are merely illusory appearances in the Real. According to Maharshi, *life in the world is not a hindrance to sustained spiritual practice since the world is only in the mind, not outside. One therefore does not have to renounce the world to follow the quest for the Self.* Neither is the spiritual practice of 'self enquiry', which requires unbroken abidance in the Self, a hindrance to the proper performance of work. *Since there is nothing other than the Self, all activity is recognized as a manifestation of the Self. Work is therefore performed with devotion and full attention, with a sense of oneness with the work and without extraneous and diverting thoughts to divert one from total absorption in the work.* All work is performed to the best of one's ability and in a selfless spirit of worship, being recognized as the activity of God or the Supreme.

At a higher philosophical level - since activity is the harmonious and dynamic manifestation of the energies of the one and infinite Self on the plane of relativity - all action is recognized as being an intrinsic property of the Self i.e. of the nature of the Self. *All action is therefore an unfolding of the Divine Will.* Advances in modern physics now express much the same view in scientific terms (Chapter 7). *The individual self is merely the instrument or channel of action.* It follows that action must proceed with less limitation, the less the instrument or channel is limited relative to the infinite Self. It is the ego sense that limits the infinite Self, and therefore the greater the ego the greater the limitation. Mahatma Gandhi expressed this philosophy of action in the following words.

"Questions do not arise for me. After all, if God guides my actions, what should I think? Why should I think? Even thought may be an obstacle in the way of His guidance." (Talks. Number 646)

The practice of abidance in the Self through the technique of 'self enquiry' gradually diminishes the ego and, in proportion to such diminution of the ego, the manifestation of the power of the Self in action is less obstructed. *Wisdom in action therefore consists in surrender to, or abidance in, the Self, as there is then no impediment to the operation of the Divine Will - the source of the power behind all action.*

"Safe, like children who embrace a pillar and whirl around it fast, those who - holding Siva firmly in the heart - live in the world never fall into delusion. They rely on God's strength, not the ego's weakness." (Guru Vachaka Kovai Saying 735)

"Upon realization that the Self is the sole Reality, actions are seen merely as phenomena that do not affect the Self. When the enlightened one acts, he has no sense of being a doer. Actions are spontaneous, and he merely remains a witness to them, without motive or attachment. The spiritual aspirant should also practice such an attitude in relation to his work, which will then cease to be a hindrance to meditation." (Talks Number 17)

"Our actions are due to a Higher Power but we think we are the originators of our actions. Action is impelled by desire and desire arises because of the rise of the ego (a sense of one's individuality). The ego however has its source in the Higher Power upon which its existence depends. It cannot remain

apart. So how can one say 'I act'. It is like a lame man boasting that he could fight the enemy if he were helped to stand up." *(Talks Number 210)*

"If work - seemingly external to oneself - does not obstruct individual awareness, it follows that performance of work - when realized to be not separate from the Self - will not obstruct one's uninterrupted awareness of the Self." *(Talks Number 454)*

"Actions themselves do not form bondage i.e. result in subjection to the law of karma. It is the false notion 'I am the doer' that is the bondage. Abandon this notion and let the body and senses play their role, unimpeded by your interference (i.e. be disinterested in the action, which must however be performed with full attention)." *(Talks Number 46)*

"It is possible to perform all the activities of life with detachment and regard only the Self as real. It is wrong to assume that if one is fixed in the Self, one's duties in life will not be properly performed. One must be like the actor who dresses and acts and even feels the part he is playing, but knows that he is not that character but someone else in real life. In the same way, why should body consciousness disturb you when once you know for certain that you are not the body but the Self. Nothing the body does should shake you from abidance in the Self." *(Day by Day with Bhagavan p.211)*

"One should engage in activity but in such a manner that bondage is weakened and not strengthened. That is self-less action." *(Talks Number 525)*

"If one realizes that one's existence is the infinite Self; that it is therefore inclusive of all that one perceives; and that there is nothing apart from or beyond it; one will not entertain desires. By not entertaining desires, one will be content." *(Talks Number 625)*

"When the Self is realized, world phenomena will be regarded with indifference. One will act in the world like an actor in a drama - free from attachment to one's role. All activity will go on as ordained by the Supreme Power. The body will complete the task for which it came into being." *(Talks Number 653)*

"Knowing your true identity, and ever in the heart abiding as the supreme Self alone, play perfectly your human role - tasting every pain and pleasure in common with all creatures." *(Guru Vachaka Kovai Saying 81)*

"When the real, effortless, permanent and happy state of the Self is realized, it is found that it is not inconsistent with the ordinary activities of life. One can live freely among people because one's true nature as the Self is peace and happiness." *(Talks Number 597)*

"He who is active in the world, remaining desire-less (unattached to action) and without losing sight of his essential nature (as the Self), is alone true to himself. It is better to do one's duty without any sense of doer-ship than to renounce action and feel that one is a 'sannyasi' i.e. one who has renounced the world." *(Talks Number 530)*

"From the point of view of 'jnana' or Reality, suffering in the world is a dream as is the world itself of which it is part. However, until you attain 'jnana' and wake out of this dream - the illusory phenomenal world - one must do social service by relieving suffering wherever one sees it. But even so, it must be done without the ego sense i.e. the feeling 'It is I who am doing it'. Instead, one should feel 'I am the Lord's instrument'. Similarly, one must not think 'I am helping a man who is inferior to me' or 'He needs help and I am in a position to do so'. You must help him as a means of worshipping God in him. All such service is serving the Self, not anybody else. You are not helping anybody else but only yourself." *(Day by Day with Bhagavan. p.80)*

> "Do not perform, as if they were worth doing, the actions that the worrying mind decides or fancies it should do. To act as you are moved to act by the grace of God, the Life of life, is the wisest form of worship true." (Guru Vachaka Kovai Saying 467)

> "As heart within the heart abiding, the Lord alone makes all things happen as ordained. Hence, if we stand unswerving and inhering in the Self, then all things will proceed unerring and unhampered." (Guru Vachaka Kovai Saying 473)

One of the important mystic insights is that activity - the constant flow of transformation and change - is an innate characteristic of the universe. We have seen that this is symbolized in the Dance of Shiva. The universe is engaged in ceaseless motion and activity, in a continual cosmic process. *Being one with the dynamic universe, inactivity on one's part, in the sense of passivity, is not possible. The term 'non-action', as used in Eastern philosophical thought, really means abstaining from activity that is out of harmony with the ongoing cosmic process i.e. action that is contrary to nature. By such non-action, one is in harmony with the cosmic process, and such action alone can be successful.*

In the mystic worldview, there are two kinds of activity viz. activity in harmony with, and activity against, the natural cosmic process. These two kinds of activity are related to two kinds of knowledge, or two modes of consciousness. One is the intuitive, which is associated with mysticism and the other the rational, which is associated with science. The two are complementary modes of functioning of the human mind. Rational thinking is linear and analytic as it belongs to the realm of the intellect, the nature of which is to discriminate and categorize. Rational knowledge thus tends to be fragmented. Intuition, on the other hand, is direct non-intellectual experience of reality arising in an expanded state of awareness. As the reality is an indivisible whole, its knowledge is holistic.

Intuitive knowledge, being born out of direct non-intellectual experience of this reality, tends to be associated with activities that are synthesizing, co-operative, contractive and responsive. Rational knowledge, on the other hand, being the product of a limited rational consciousness, is associated with activities that are analytic, competitive, demanding and aggressive. *Western science and society has consistently and heavily favoured rational knowledge over intuitive wisdom, and it is this profound imbalance between the two modes of consciousness that lies at the heart of the crisis that besets the world today.*

The strong preference for the values and attitudes associated with rational knowledge has resulted in a society where the social, educational, economic and political institutions are mutually reinforcing. Society is therefore blind to the dangers that activities motivated by these values and attitudes create. The way of Nature is however a harmonious balance between the values and attitudes associated with both types of knowledge. The activities of our so-called 'modern' society violate the way of nature, and it should therefore not be a matter of surprise that the world today faces several critical problems.

Rational thinking, as pointed out earlier, is linear whereas holistic awareness springs from an intuitive 'feel' for non-linear systems. One of the most difficult things for people in a culture dominated by rational, linear and analytic thinking to comprehend is that if one does something that is good, or if something is good, then more of the same will not necessarily be better. We therefore think it a hallmark of success if we can do things faster; continuously increase our level of material comforts; and use more and more of the finite resources of the planet without a thought for the needs of future generations. *Like the abject reliance that primitive peoples placed in the spiritual powers of shamans and wizards for solutions to their problems, the rationalists of today imagine that scientific and technical progress can solve all the problems that they create by activities contrary to the workings of nature. It is also a belief in magic, but magic of an unattractive kind that denies a place to the human spirit.*

It is as a result of the dominance of such rationalist thinking over intuition, over the past three centuries, that the world today faces a crisis involving several interlinked problems. There are armed conflicts and terrorist attacks; increasing poverty associated with widening of the gap between 'haves' and 'have-nots'; ruthless exploitation of finite natural resources; environmental degradation both by such exploitation and technologies that cause widespread air and water pollution; and destruction of natural biodiversity and natural ecosystems on an unprecedented scale. In the 'developed' countries, where the dominance of rationalism is most marked, there is a particularly marked increase in the incidence of chronic, degenerative illnesses such as heart disease and cancer; in social disintegration manifested in a sharp rise in psychiatric disorders, violent crime, suicides, and drug abuse; and severe air and water pollution. *All these problems have arisen and continue to flourish because of the striking disparity between the emphasis placed on scientific knowledge, technological skills and self-interest, and the simultaneous neglect of true intuitive wisdom, spirituality, and ethics based on a sense of oneness with the world and all its beings.* Judging by the sad state of the world, it is no exaggeration to assert that this one-sided evolution has now reached a stage where it borders insanity.

The imbalance in our attitude towards rational and intuitive knowledge is rooted in a narrow and mistaken perception of the true reality, based on the philosophy behind the, now out-dated, Cartesian worldview. Different facets of this mis-perception - which formed the basis of classical science - are the view of the universe as a mechanical system composed of separate, elementary 'building blocks'; the notion of the body also as a physical machine and apart from the surrounding world; the view of life in society as a competitive struggle for existence; the belief in unlimited material progress, - achieved through technological and economic growth - as the purpose of life on earth; belief in the scientific method as the only valid approach to knowledge; the supremacy of the human mind; the mistaken concept of God as a person; and an equally mistaken and degraded vision of one's own identity.

The problems faced by us today can only be overcome if they are recognized to be systemic problems i.e. closely interconnected elements in an indivisible whole. They cannot be understood and resolved within the fragmented approach that is intrinsic to the Cartesian perception of reality held in the traditional Western worldview. This approach merely shifts them around in the complex web of social and ecological relations that is the true nature of reality. The problems can be resolved only if the structure of the web is changed, and this demands that our values as well as social, economic and political institutions are transformed. Cloaking ourselves in technological glory can never solve anything fundamental.

A basis for such transformation is provided by the new vision of reality, now shared alike by both Eastern mysticism and science. The vision demands profound personal as well as cultural transformation, to accord with a radical change in our perception of our true nature; our true relationship to the world; and the true purpose of our life on earth. The altogether new outlook would form the basis, not only of a changed personal approach to daily life and its problems, but also of future social institutions, economic systems and technologies. All of them would be such as would intertwine to produce a peaceful, harmonious, interdependent and sustainable world order.

The most important feature in the new outlook or vision is that the world is seen as an integrated whole rather than as a collection of separate parts. This outlook has been called *'deep ecological awareness'* because, as in ecology, it is an awareness that recognizes the fundamental interdependence and unity of all events and phenomena, and embedded-ness of all parts (individuals, institutions and societies) in one indivisible whole. Such an awareness - which was embodied in 'sanathana dharma' or the perennial philosophy of Hinduism - is now supported by modern science. Its basis is an intuitive perception of reality that goes beyond the framework of conventional science to awareness of the one-ness of all life; of the interdependence of its manifold manifestations because of self-consistency of the whole; and of its cycles of change and transformation. Ultimately therefore, deep ecological awareness is spiritual awareness. *When the human spirit - the true self of the individual - is understood to be the mode of consciousness in which it is none other than the Supreme Spirit or Infinite, Eternal Consciousness - the substratum and source of the cosmos - it becomes clear that deep ecological awareness is spiritual in its deepest essence.* [45]

The perennial spiritual philosophy embodied in Hinduism and the other derived Eastern religions thus provides the most consistent spiritual background to the new vision of science. *The best approach to the development of deep ecological awareness and action in accordance with such awareness is therefore spiritual development. A direct and scientific path for achieving this goal has been provided by Ramana Maharshi.* This is the topic of the next chapter.

CHAPTER 9

THE PATH TO TRUTH

Science, in its purest form is natural philosophy and its aim is to unravel the mysteries of nature. The progress of science however fostered a materialistic outlook, and an emphasis on rationalism - leading to the myth of incompatibility between the objective, rational knowledge of science and the subjective, intuitive knowledge associated with spirituality. The Eastern religious philosophies, and religions in general, were relegated to the background as being irrational or mere subjective speculation. They were considered to have little relevance to the practicalities of life in the modern world.

Sub-atomic research into the fundamental nature of matter, beginning in the early years of the 20th century, has however now led science to a worldview that is closely similar to that of the ancient Eastern religious philosophies. Matter, at its most fundamental level, is not solid physical substance but a manifestation of energy. *In reality therefore, the essence of the universe is spiritual (non-substance) rather than material (substance). On the basis of its most recent research, subatomic physics has even begun to recognize that a Cosmic Consciousness may be the ultimate essence of the universe.*

A universal, eternal Supreme Consciousness as the cause and substance of the universe has been the central doctrine of all Eastern religions. It is a doctrine based on direct knowledge of the Reality in mystic experience, just as scientific knowledge is based on experiments and observations on nature. In Hinduism, this Supreme Consciousness has been called Brahman or Paramatman; in Buddhism the Dharmakeya; and in Taoism the Tao. **The universe is seen merely as a**

manifestation or appearance in an absolute reality that is of the nature of pure, eternal and infinite Consciousness.

In Advaita Vedanta, the highest philosophical expression of the ancient Vedic religion, the essential nature of reality is eternal, infinite and non-dual Existence. Defining reality as the unchanging and eternal substratum underlying things that change, it asserts that 'existence' is the reality. The things we perceive are particular modes of existence or transient presentations that cannot exist but for the underlying 'existence' that is imperishable and absolute. This 'existence', according to Vedanta, is of the nature of awareness or intelligence. The reality is therefore pure existence and pure consciousness. It is not mere inert substance. It alone is self-existent - a fundamental criterion of reality - since it alone is illumined by its own nature.

As there is no duality in the Reality, any perception of diversity is illusory. Most philosophical schools and religions however postulate the separate existence and reality of three entities viz. God, the individual soul and a material world. According to Advaita Vedanta, such a perception is only real at the level of relativity, which is the standpoint or perspective of the ego, i.e. one's sense of limited individual existence. At a higher or absolutist level i.e. from the standpoint, if it may be so called, of the true reality of Brahman the Absolute, the three are mere appearances therein. They are really one and identical with Brahman. It follows therefore that, to comprehend the absolute truth or reality, one must destroy one's sense of ego. This was the central and persistent teaching of Maharshi.

"All systems of thought postulate three principles (i.e. the world, souls and God). Only one principle appears as three principles. To say that the three principles ever remain as three principles is only so long as the ego lasts. After the destruction of the ego, to remain in one's own state is best." (Verse 2. Forty Verses on Reality)

"Apart from thought, there is no soul (jiva), God or world. With every thought, the 'I' thought (ego) is admixed. It is the origin of every thought. The place where this arises is the Heart - the Self." (Guru Vachaka Kovai Saying 449)

The Path of Self Enquiry

The technique prescribed by Maharshi to destroy one's ego and thereby arrive at the truth or reality of oneself and of all else was that of 'self-enquiry' It enables one, by assiduous practice, to give up the deeply ingrained idea that there is an individual self which functions through the body and mind. *The method and goal of self-enquiry are the same viz. to abide in the source of the mind and to be what one really is.* Maharshi made it the basis of a spiritual philosophy and associated practical spiritual discipline, just as the Four Noble Truths and the Noble Eightfold Path are the spiritual philosophy and practical discipline of the teaching of the Buddha. Maharshi's spiritual philosophy, in its practical aspect, is best expressed in the following verses from his 'Forty Verses on Reality'.

"Leaving out the seeing self, oneself seeing God is but seeing a mental image. (If it is asked) 'Does he, at least who sees the self, see God?' (The answer is) 'How can one see after one's head is lost? For the self is not other than God!'." (Verse 20. Forty Verses on Reality)

"If it be asked 'What is the truth of the scriptural texts which speak of oneself seeing the Self and seeing God?' (The reply is) 'Since oneself is one, how can oneself see oneself? If one's Self cannot be seen, how can God be seen? Getting absorbed is seeing'." (Verse 21. Forty Verses on Reality)

"Lending light (awareness) to the mind, (the Lord or Supreme Consciousness) shines in the mind. Other than by turning the mind inwards and lodging it in the Lord, how is it possible to

think of the Lord with the mind." (Verse 22. *Forty Verses on Reality*)

In the first of the above set of three verses, it is declared that *the seeing of God, with form, is merely a seeing by the mind of an image projected by itself.* This teaching conforms to the current view, now held both in modern physics and Eastern spirituality, that all visual impressions depend on the observer's mind and senses, both for their perception and interpretation. To the question whether in realizing the Self one sees God with form, the answer is that this is not possible. This follows from two facts viz. that the ego or finite mind that 'sees' has its source in the infinite Existence-Awareness that is the Self, and that God is - in reality - this Self. In Self-realization, the ego or mind loses itself in its source, and consequently no relationships such as 'seer-seeing-seen' or 'subject-object' are possible in this state. *God therefore cannot be visually seen when the Self is realized.*

The second and third verses elaborate on this theme. Since the Self or sole Reality is an indivisible unity, the seeing of the Self in a dualistic subject-object relationship is impossible. As God is not other than this non-dual Self, objective seeing of God is also impossible. *So when one speaks of seeing God, it really means realizing one's true identity as the Self or God by absorption in the Self. Seeing is not visual seeing but being the Self. This happens when the ego or mind disappears by merging in the Self.* Therefore, if the mind is to comprehend God, it must turn inwards, away from the world, and merge or lodge itself in its source, the Self or God.

The third verse also points out that *the power of the mind to know anything is due to the Self (God), which alone is the source of all awareness. The Self or God does not stand outside the mind since there is no 'outside' for the non-dual Self.* It is the very ground, source and basis of the mind. The mind however usually goes outwards through the senses, sees an outside and therefore fails to see the Self that is its source.

The only way the mind can know the Self or God is therefore for it to turn inwards and be absorbed in its source - the Self.

"This body will not say 'I'. In sleep, nobody says 'I am not'. After the ego 'I' rises, all rise. Therefore enquire with a keen mind from where this 'I' rises." *(Verse 23. Forty Verses on Reality)*

"The inert body will not say 'I'. The Existence-Consciousness will not rise. The 'I' of the measure of the body rises in between the two. This is called the knot of the intelligent and inert; bondage; the individual soul; the subtle body; the ego; the mind; transmigration. Thus should you know." *(Verse 24. Forty Verses on Reality)*

"Grasping a form, it rises. Grasping a form it stands. Grasping a form it eats and waxes; leaving a form it grasps another form. When sought, it takes to flight – this shapeless and ghostly ego!" *(Verse 25. Forty Verses on Reality)*

"If the ego is, all else is. If the ego is not, all else is not. The ego, verily, is all. Therefore the enquiry as to what it is, merely means the giving up of all." *(Verse 26. Forty Verses on Reality)*

In the first of this set of four verses, it is pointed out that in the state of sleep, we do not deny our existence despite the absence of ego consciousness (our sense of individuality). This implies that we are conscious of our existence in that state. *There is therefore an unbroken Consciousness beyond ego consciousness, which is absent in sleep but upon the rise of which the body and the world appear.* The intermittent ego consciousness (the ego 'I') is unreal, as one of the criteria for reality is unbroken existence, and the ego consciousness is absent in sleep. We are therefore enjoined to probe into the source of the unreal ego 'I' as this source must be the real Awareness from which the ego 'I' rises. As the mind is merely an expansion of the ego 'I' through thought, such inquiry amounts to the mind searching for its own ground.

The second verse declares that the ego 'I' - the 'I' notion or sense of individual limited existence - cannot belong to the physical body since it is inert. Neither can it be the real Self, because the real Self is eternal and infinite Existence-Consciousness, unlimited and unchanging. *The ego 'I' is an illusion appearing in the waking state as a result of the superimposition of the awareness of the Self upon a finite and inert body.* For believers in Advaita, it does not matter by what name it is called - the soul, the subtle body, the ego, the mind, bondage or that which reincarnates - since there is, in reality, only the one non-dual Self. *What seems to be other than the Self is merely an appearance in the Self and it does not matter by what name it is called.*

The next two verses amplify on the nature of the ego 'I'. The first of these emphasizes that it cannot exist, function or survive without assuming a bodily form - gross or subtle. It has no form of its own and so when one inquires closely into its nature, it turns out to be an illusion. It flourishes by claiming as its own, all the thoughts and actions that accompany its appearance. *So long as the ego is taken to be real, the true Self is veiled. Upon the realization that it is unreal, the veil is lifted, and the Self then shines alone.*

The second verse points out that the manifold world appears during the waking state, when the ego 'I' appears, and disappears in sleep when the ego 'I' also disappears. In a sense therefore, the ego is all i.e. the world in all its plurality. But it is so only so long as one does not inquire into the true nature of the ego. *Such inquiry reveals that the ego arises from the pure Awareness that is the true Self When the Self - the source of the ego as well as the world appearance - is thus realized, both the ego and the world vanish.* The search for the ego amounts to the extinction of the world appearance.

"The state where the 'I' does not rise is the state where we are That (the Reality or true Self). Without seeking the place where the 'I' does not rise, how is one to attain self-loss, consisting in the non-rise of the 'I'? Without attaining self-loss, how is one to abide in one's own (true) state where one is That." (Verse 27. Forty Verses on Reality)

"When the mind, turned inwards, enquires 'Who am I?' and reaches the Heart, that which is 'I' sinks crestfallen and the one Reality appears of its own accord as 'I'. Though it appears thus, this 'I' is not an object. It is the whole. That, verily, is the Self that is the (sole) reality." (Verse 30. Forty Verses on Reality)

By seeking the source of the ego, one therefore puts an end to the ego. This state where the ego does not rise is the state where we are the non-dual Self or pure Awareness, eternal and infinite. It is our natural state, to attain which the source of the unreal ego 'I' must be sought. As the inquiring mind approaches the core or essence of one's being (called the Heart), *the unreal ego 'I' gradually disappears and the true 'I' or Self appears in its place, of its own accord. It is experienced as pure unconditioned awareness - described as 'I-I' to distinguish it from the ego 'I'. This Awareness is the substance of the real Self, which is the sole reality.* It is therefore the Whole, apart from which there is nothing else.

"To jump about and play vile tricks like a little Satan; to flit from thought to thought; to look and see and suffer much - this is the false jiva's nature. The Self's true nature is but to be and shine." (Guru Vachaka Kovai Saying 154)

Mind

Understanding the true nature of the mind is central to the practice of self-enquiry since the aim of the enquiry is to discover, by direct experience, that the mind is non-existent.

According to Maharshi, all conscious activities of the physical body and mind are based on the assumption that there is an individual 'I' responsible for them. The ego is this notion of an individual personality, and he called it the 'I' thought to convey the concept that it is a mental mode or modification of the true 'I' or the Self. *Mind is merely an expansion, through thought activity, of the ego or 'I' thought.* Maharshi often went as far as to say that the mind is only the 'I' thought. Since in the true state of the Self that is sought through self-enquiry there is no sense of individuality, it implies that its attainment involves the disappearance of the ego or mind, and their root, the 'I' thought.

"The mind is only a projection from the Self that appears in the waking state. It is a phantom proceeding from the Self, i.e. it has no reality of its own. Its destruction is therefore the non-recognition of it as something apart from the Self." (Talks Number 76)

"Mind is a projection from the Self, which appears because of the 'I' thought. If one seeks wherefrom this thought arises, it disappears into an infinitely expanded 'I' consciousness. The 'I' thought is this Consciousness, but limited." (Talks Number 489)

"The ego is the root of the mind. The (expanse of) mind arises through the thought activity of the outward turned ego consciousness of the waking state. These thoughts cause the perception or inference of a real outside world. The apparent reality of the world is thus created by the ego when it emerges, and it disappears when the ego subsides - allowing the true Consciousness to shine forth." (Talks Number 25)

"Once we admit our existence, we cannot deny our Self. Our notion that we do not know our Self is because of thoughts i.e. the mind. It is mind therefore that stands between and veils our true nature as the Self." (Talks Number 146)

"The mind is only a multitude of thoughts. All of them have their root in the 'I' thought. Whoever investigates the origin of the 'I' thought, for him the ego ('I' thought) perishes. This is true investigation. The true 'I' then shines by itself." (Talks. Number 222)

"It is habit that makes us believe that it is difficult to cease thinking. But in the natural state of the Self, where there is nothing apart from the Self, thoughts cannot arise since there is no object to be thought of." (Talks Number 398)

"One can never find the mind through the mind. One must pass beyond it in order to find that it is non-existent. The mind is only an aggregate of thoughts that cannot exist but for the ego Seek wherefrom this ego – the 'I' thought – arises and what remains over, after the disappearance of all thought, is Pure Consciousness. The mind is merely the Pure Consciousness that has put on limitations." (Talks Number 473)

"One ignores what is real and holds on to the unreal mind. As it is unreal, search for it is fruitless. Seek the reality - the Self - and the mind will be found to be unreal. It will disappear." (Talks Number 238)

"Mind is impure because of its content of thoughts. As a result of meditation or self-enquiry, it becomes the enduring background free from thoughts. This expanse of mind free from thought i.e. mind in its purity, is the Self." (Talks Number 293)

"The Self is the expanse of consciousness (chidvyoman) as distinguished from the mind, which is the expanse of thought." (chittavyoman; Talks Number 16)

"The eternal Self (also called the Heart) is the underlying principle that gives rise to, and sustains, the mind. It is the source from which thoughts arise, on which they subsist, and where they are resolved. Thoughts are the content of the mind and shape the universe. We however confound the mind with

the Self. If the source of the mind is sought, it vanishes, leaving the Self." (Talks Number 97)

"Lapsing from the Self - the seat, the Being-Awareness, vast unbroken - a separate 'I' springs up, which falls into the error of confronting a world perceived as something other than the Self." (Guru Vachaka Kovai Saying 156)

"When, with the keen unceasing quest of 'Who am I?' one penetrates the centre of oneself, the body bound ego fades away and true Being rises up as 'I'-'I', and puts an end to all the diversity that is as illusory as the blueness of the sky." (Guru Vachaka Kovai Saying 385)

"The jiva searching 'Who in truth am I?' subsides as the true Self without an 'I'" (Guru Vachaka Kovai Saying 388)

"The world and attachments to the world (born of a sense of imperfection) are of the mind and not of the Self. Thus, in the state of deep sleep, where we exist (as the Self) but the mind is dormant, there is no world, no attachments nor desires." (Talks Number 280)

"Thoughts, both good and bad, take you further away from the Self because the Self is more intimate than thoughts. Thoughts must all disappear in the Self." (Talks Number 341)

"The mind comprises both the objects seen as well as the light of awareness by which they are seen. If the objects disappear, then the light of awareness alone remains. This is the Self." (Talks Number 404)

As the Self is the only existing reality, the 'I' thought is merely a mistaken assumption with no real existence of its own. It only appears to exist, and it does so by identifying and associating with thoughts and bodily activities, and claiming them as its own, e.g. 'I think', 'I act' etc. *There is really no separate 'I' thought that exists independently of such identifications. Its apparently continuous and real existence is the result of the continuous flow of identifications. Almost all these identifications trace back to the original false assumption that one's self or 'I' is limited to the body.* This 'I am the body' notion is the root cause of all the subsequent identifications and its dissolution is therefore the primary aim of self-enquiry.

Self-enquiry attempts to check such identifications by isolating the 'I' thought. Attention is focused on the subjective feeling of 'I am', so that associative thoughts such as 'I think', 'I act' etc do not have a chance to rise. Since the 'I thought' is now no longer able to make the identifications or connections that give it an apparently continuous existence, it withers away and finally disappears. In its place there arises the direct experience of the true 'I am' or the Self. It may be said that the 'I' thought dissolves in its source - the pure unconditioned 'being' of the Self. *Self-enquiry may therefore also be described as the discipline of constant attention to the inner awareness or 'I am' until it is merged in its source.* The ego's apparent phenomenal existence is transcended when one dives into the source from where the 'I' thought rises. Maharshi maintained that this was the most direct means of discovering the unreality of the 'I' thought and thereby attaining its source, the true 'I' or Self. All other spiritual disciplines are therefore auxiliaries or preliminaries to that of self-enquiry.

"Under whatever name and in whatever form the omnipresent, nameless and formless reality is worshipped, that is only a door to realization. Understanding one's own truth in the truth of that true reality and being one with it, having been resolved into it, is (alone) true seeing (of the reality). Thus should you know." (Verse 8. Forty Verses on Reality)

"God is hearsay but one's existence is directly experienced. One should only make use of direct experience and therefore one must enquire 'Who am 'I'?' Without wasting time on polemics, one should therefore engage in the above enquiry.

Turn the mind inward and spend the time usefully." (Talks. Number 332)

"The body and the world are all thoughts, which owe their rise to the 'I' thought. If the 'I' thought is held, all other thoughts will disappear. The 'I' thought will also finally vanish leaving the Self in its purity, as it alone is real. There will then be no body, mind or ego. They disappear because they are not real." (Talks. Number 244)

"Unfailing immortality accrues only to those who have destroyed the ego, whose demon dance obstructs the vision of the precious truth that we are the ever-perfect Being-Awareness-Bliss." (Guru Vachaka Kovai Saying 225)

"Beside the Self, nothing in truth exists. But then the deep delusion that the body is oneself makes one let go the permanent, non-dual bliss of immortality and fall into birth and death." (Guru Vachaka Kovai Saying 615)

The practice of self-enquiry is different from all forms of traditional meditation since these necessitate the existence of a subject that concentrates on an object of thought. Duality is perpetuated. Such a relationship actually sustains the subject viz. the sense of individuality or 'I' thought, instead of contributing to its disappearance, which is the aim of self-enquiry. Such meditation cannot possibly lead to attainment of one's true state - the state of the Self - which is one of non-duality and where, therefore, all perception ceases. This can take place only by disappearance of the subject 'I'. *At best, all other forms of meditation are therefore to be regarded merely as preliminaries or stages in the practice of self-enquiry.* They only serve to quieten the mind, but can never lead to Self-realization since the 'I' thought is not being isolated and attenuated, leading to its eventual disappearance.

"Barring fruitful self-enquiry, there is - for real mind control - no other sadhana whatsoever. The mind may seem to be

controlled by other methods; but after a while, it will spring up again." (Guru Vachaka Kovai, Saying 756)

"Meditation differs according to the degree of advancement of the seeker. If one is ready for it, one should directly hold the thinker (the ego or 'I' thought). The thinker will then subside into his source – Pure Consciousness Less advanced seekers should meditate on God, and this will bestow on them the fitness to hold the thinker." (Talks. Number 453)

"Meditation is objective in its approach whereas self-enquiry is subjective. As the latter seeks to eschew unreality and arrive at the reality, it is scientific." (Talks. Number 338)

The practice of self-enquiry also differs from other forms of meditation in that it is not a repressive method of controlling the mind. It is a gentle technique that, in its earlier stages, requires uninterrupted awareness of the 'I' thought, so that one is led to its source. It is not a forcible exercise in concentration or suppression of thoughts. One merely withdraws attention from thoughts other than the 'I' thought. *Both the method and the goal of self-enquiry are the same - to abide in the source of the mind and thus be aware of one's true nature as pure consciousness. So long as effort is required, it is self-enquiry; but when it is spontaneous and natural, it is the goal viz. realization.*

Not being based on a subject-object approach, it is strictly not a meditation practice. While regular periods of formal practice are recommended for beginners, it should ideally be carried out throughout one's waking hours, irrespective of what one is doing. This becomes possible with regular practice, so that there is really no conflict between working and self-enquiry. One therefore does not have to give up one's usual duties in the world. It is merely abidance in one's real nature irrespective what one is doing – requiring effort at first but later becoming effortless.

"Work - performed with the notion that it is external to oneself - does not obstruct individual awareness. It therefore follows that work - when performed with the conviction that it is not separate from one's true self - will not obstruct uninterrupted awareness of the Self." (Talks Number 454)

The technique of self-enquiry is the only spiritual discipline that does not depend on the mind (ego). Since all other disciplines require it as their instrument, they cannot bring about its permanent disappearance and thus enable one to realize one's true nature as the absolute, unconditioned consciousness or Self. Experience of Reality is simply the loss of the ego and self-enquiry is the only practice that directly achieves this objective.

"One ignores what is real and holds on to the unreal mind. (It is unreal because it is impermanent - being absent in sleep). Searching for unreality is fruitless. Thinking that one is the mind, one seeks to check the mind (by meditation etc). There is only one way to rule over the mind and that is by directly seeking the reality - the Self." (Talks. Number 238)

"One must first develop humility and an open mind before one can embark on the path of self-enquiry. Only then will one listen and try to understand the instruction imparted." (Talks. Number 645)

"One can never find the (true nature of) mind through the mind. One must pass beyond it in order to find that is non-existent. The mind is only an aggregate of thoughts that cannot exist but for the ego Seek wherefrom this ego or 'I thought' rises. What remains over, after the disappearance of all thought, is Pure Consciousness. The mind is merely the Pure Consciousness that has taken on limitations." (Talks. Number 473)

"Mind is impure and restless because of its content of thought (which takes it away from its true nature as Self or Pure Consciousness). As a result of meditation or self-enquiry, it

The Path to Truth

becomes the enduring background free from thoughts. This expanse of mind devoid of thought i.e. mind in its pristine purity, is the Self." (Talks Number 293)

"Instead of setting about saying that there is a mind and it must be destroyed, one must begin to seek the source of the mind. The mind, turned outwards, results in thoughts and the world Turned inwards, it becomes itself the Self." (Day by Day with Bhagavan p.31)

"None can confront and overcome the mind. Ignore it, then, as something false, unreal. Know the Self as the real ground, and stand firm-rooted in it. Then the mind's movements will gradually subside." (Guru Vachaka Kovai Saying 921)

"The Self can be known only by experiencing that state (of being the Self) because that state has no limits, whereas our present state (of consciousness) is limited. The limited (mind) cannot comprehend the unlimited (Self). Its understanding of the Self can only be according to its (limited) capacity." (Talks. Number 445)

Among the various forms of meditation upon God, Maharshi regarded meditation in the 'ananya bhava' mode as the best. 'Ananya' means 'not other', as opposed to 'anya' which means 'other', and therefore this form of meditation is non-dual in nature - involving meditation upon God as none other than one's self. All other forms of meditation upon God are in the 'anya bhava' mode i.e. they involve meditation upon God as other than one's self. *Since one's self, alone, is 'ananya', i.e. not other than oneself, even the thought 'He am I' is 'anya' i.e. other than oneself.* Meditation in the 'ananya bhava' mode therefore implies meditation upon God as 'That which shines with one as 'I' viz. the reality of the first person. It is not meditation on the thought 'He am I', but the firm conviction 'He am I' is an essential pre-requisite for meditation in the 'ananya bhava'. It is consequently appropriate only for those who accept unconditionally the philosophy of Advaita Vedanta.

When one completely withdraws attention from what is 'other' and meditates upon 'I' (the reality of oneself), one's sense of individuality (the ego) will wither, since individuality can persist only so long as one attends to what is 'other' i.e. other than oneself. *The final outcome of meditation in the 'ananya bhava' mode is therefore the subsidence of the ego (who is the meditator) in its source. This is the state of Pure Being or Existence-Consciousness.*

Since the meditator becomes non-existent when this subsidence takes place, no further meditation is possible and the state of Pure Being is therefore described as 'bhavanatita' i.e. beyond meditation. According to Maharshi, abidance in this state is supreme devotion to God, since God is, in truth, nothing other than this state of Pure Being - the real Self.

"Abidance in the state of Being that transcends thought and devotion, by the strength of one's meditation, is the truth of supreme devotion." (Verse 9. Upadesa Saram)

"Since God is the Self in one's Heart (the reality of one's being), constant meditation on the truth of oneself is the type of meditation most pleasing to Him." (Guru Ramana Vachana Malai. 107)

"Devotion to God as the real self is the highest devotion. It leads to quiescence of mind and merging of the ego in God, the Real Self. This is the truth of offering one's self to God, which devotees are enjoined to perform." (Guru Ramana Vachana Malai. 112)

"It is said that meditation on one's own being is supreme devotion to all-transcending God. This is so because, though spoken of as two, they are in substance one." (Guru Vachaka Kovai Saying 730)

The Path to Truth

"Perfect devotion is just the persistence of identity with the One – the all-embracing Reality – that shines forth when the false 'I' (ego) is utterly destroyed by the quest for the Self." (Guru Ramana Vachana Malai. 123)

Meditation in the 'ananya bhava' leads to submergence of the ego (as meditator) in its source – the Self or state of Pure Being – while self-enquiry results in the disappearance of the ego (as thinker) in the same source. The two practices are therefore not very different since they lead to achievement of the same objective. The former is however more acceptable to those who believe in a personal God, while the latter appeals to more advanced aspirants who are able to accept God as impersonal.

"Meditation is the inner attitude that one is but the Self Supreme that shines as Being-Awareness-Bliss. Self-enquiry is making the mind abide firm in the Self until the false ego – iilusion's seed – has perished." (Guru Vachaka Kovai Saying 738)

Explaining how the technique of self-enquiry leads to realization of the Self, Maharshi described the ego as a blend between the Self, which is pure consciousness, and the physical body, which is inert and insentient. *In investigating or diving into the source of the ego, one holds on to its essential consciousness aspect, and for this reason the enquiry must lead to realization of the pure consciousness of the Self.* In an apt analogy, the consciousness aspect of the ego is compared to the scent of a dog's master in his clothing, - which unfailingly reunites the dog with its master.

"The ego (in the form of 'aham vritti') functions as the knot between consciousness and the inert body. In your investigation into its source, you take the essential consciousness aspect of the ego and for this reason self-enquiry must lead to realization of the pure consciousness of the Self." (Maharshi's Gospel pp. 83-85)

Since the 'I' thought, the root of the mind, merges into the pure consciousness of the Self as a result of self-enquiry, the essence of mind - according to Maharshi - is only awareness or consciousness. When it dominated and limited by the ego, it functions as the sensing, thinking or reasoning faculties. The pure mind, not being limited by the ego, has nothing separate from itself and so is only aware. This is the true implication of the biblical statement 'I am that I AM'. *One's true nature is pure consciousness.*

"The Self is pure consciousness in the state of sleep. It evolves as aham ('I') without the idam (this) in the transition stage (between sleep and waking). Upon complete waking, it manifests as aham ('I') and idam (this). The individual's experience is by means of aham ('I') only. Realization can therefore only be by means of the transitional 'I'. If the transitional 'I' is realized, the substratum is found and that leads to the goal. (Being pure, it alone can merge into the pure and infinite consciousness that is the Self (Brahman) - which is not possible for the impure 'I' of the waking state)." (Talks. Number 314)

In essence, the discipline or practice of self-enquiry involves being attentive to the inner feeling of 'I' or 'I' thought, without interruption. Whenever attention is distracted by other thoughts, it must be turned back to the 'I' thought. As any such thought arose, Maharshi suggested that one should ask oneself 'Who am I?' or 'Where does this inner feeling of 'I' come from?' This transfers attention from thoughts to the thinker.

"Breaks in pure awareness are due to thoughts. Awareness of the breaks is also a thought. One should therefore repeat the question 'To whom does this thought arise?' and keep it up until there is continuity of pure awareness." (Talks. Number 628)

"To enquire 'Who am I?' really means trying to find out the source of the ego or 'I' thought. Seeking the source of the 'I'

thought serves as a means of getting rid of all other thoughts. As each thought rises, one asks 'To whom does this thought arise?' As the answer will be 'I get the thought', one continues the enquiry by asking 'Who is this 'I' and what is its source?'." (Day by Day with Bhagavan. p.68)

"*A strong conviction that one is truly the Self that transcends the mind and phenomena is an essential pre-requisite for successful effort in self-enquiry. One must hold the Self even during mental activities.*" *(Talks. Number 406)*

"*The spiritual practice of self-enquiry consists in withdrawal within the Self every time one is disturbed by a thought. It is not concentration or destruction of the mind but withdrawal into the Self.*" *(Talks Number 485)*

"*If the mind - turned outward and distracted - starts observing its own being, then alienation ends; the vestige ego merges in the light of true Awareness shining in the heart.*" *(Guru Vachaka Kovai Saying 193)*

In the early stages of self-enquiry, paying attention to the 'I' thought is a mental activity requiring effort. The 'I' thought is held in the form of a thought or perception Gradually however, the thought of the 'I' gives way to an intuitive feeling of 'I' As one holds on to it without interruption, this subjectively experienced feeling of 'I' ceases to connect with thoughts or objects and disappears. What remains is a blissful experience of being, in which the sense of individuality has temporarily ceased to operate. This experience is intermittent at first, but with practice it becomes easier and easier to attain and maintain. When one reaches this stage, there is effortless awareness of pure being. Individual effort is now no longer possible as the 'I' (the ego) that made the effort in the earlier stages has temporarily ceased to exist. From then on, it is more a process of effortless being than an effort to be. Repeated experience of this state of pure being weakens the 'vasanas' or mental tendencies that cause the 'I' thought to manifest. When their hold has been sufficiently weakened, the power of the Self destroys them so completely that the 'I' thought never rises again. This is the final and irreversible state of Self-realization.

"Thoughts cast a veil over the Reality. There is no thought in the state of realization; there is only the feeling 'I am'. This feeling, the ego-less 'I am', is not a thought. It is the state of realization. The experience of 'I am' is being still." (Talks. Number 226)

"Self-realization is merely a euphemism for elimination of ignorance. It is a very direct experience, - it is 'being' the Self, not any feeling about the Self." (Talks. Number 500)

"Our existence, which we cannot deny, is the Self. It is pure Consciousness. So we are always 'realized'. The effort to realize is therefore merely the effort to realize our present mistake (ignorance) that we have not realized our Self." (Talks. Number 625)

"Realization is not the acquisition of anything new or the gaining of a new faculty. It is merely the removal of the camouflage (of wrong knowledge) that veiled the reality. The wrong knowledge is the assumption 'I am the body'. Because this limitation has been wrongly assumed, it must be transcended. There is nothing to be gained anew. Realization is nothing more than being in one's pristine state." (Talks. Numbers 63, 96)

"The one infinite, eternal, unbroken whole that is the Self is aware of itself as 'I'. This 'I' is always experienced, yet attention has to be drawn to this truth (because the experience is clouded over by the false notion of individuality). The real purpose of all religions and scriptures is to draw one's attention to this truth." (Talks. Number 92)

"Whether the world is perceived as real or else conceptual and unreal, you - the Knower - are there, are you not, as Awareness

present? Such Being, as pure awareness is the Self." (Guru Vachaka Kovai Saying 1035)

"Since one cannot deny one's existence at any time - even in sleep when the intellect is absent - there is no point of time when one is not realized. One's very existence is realization." (Talks. Number 477)

"Everyone experiences the Self (Pure Awareness). The experience of the 'ajnani' is clouded by his 'vasanas', whereas that of the 'jnani' is not so. The latter's experience of the Self is clear and permanent. The 'ajnani', after long practice, may gain a glimpse of the Self, but because of resurgence of the old 'vasanas' the experience is not permanent. Practice must be continued until they are completely destroyed. He will then be able to remain permanently in his real state. The glimpse is an incentive to such further effort." (Talks. Number 562)

"The state of the Self - the highest state - is the same. The experience is also the same. But interpretation of the experience is made with the mind. Minds are different and so interpretations are different. Interpretations also differ according to the circumstances and the nature of the seekers." (Talks. Number 595)

The spiritual philosophy of Advaita Vedanta is based on direct insight into the true nature of reality. Such insight is absolute or holistic knowledge, in contrast to the relative and fragmented knowledge of science and sensory perception. Maharshi's method of self-enquiry provides us with a direct and simple means to gain such insight for ourselves, divorced from all dry philosophical speculation and arguments about reality. All that one needs to embark on the quest for such insight is mental flexibility or open-ness of mind to new ideas; intellectual conviction of the validity of Advaita philosophy; and the will and consuming desire to pursue the quest until insight into the true nature of reality is gained.

Attachment to dogma and the resultant unwillingness to alter one's beliefs are perhaps the major obstacles to following the path of self-enquiry. In any field of endeavour, progress is not possible unless one is willing to accept change. *Progress in science itself has been due to willingness to alter or abandon previously held concepts as soon as they seemed inadequate to explain new phenomena. Similarly, to make progress in the search for truth or reality, one must hold one's current beliefs as to its nature as tentative, and be prepared to change them if it seems reasonable or desirable to do so.*

"Though ardently we study immaculate works of radiant wisdom, yet - as through meditation we make these gains our own - we must forget and leave behind what once we learnt."
(Guru Vachaka Kovai Saying 147)

Intellectual conviction of the validity of pure Advaita Vedanta is now much easier, since the elements of this philosophy provide a consistent and relevant framework for the theories of modern science. The conception of the world, the beliefs and the spiritual aims of this philosophy are in perfect harmony with recent scientific discoveries. In the preceding chapters, the parallels and convergence between the theories of modern science and the principles of Advaita Vedanta have been elaborated upon. *Pure Advaita does not conflict with the philosophy of modern science, in contrast to Judaea-Christian philosophy that does.*

If one concedes that science, in its essence, is the search for the truth or reality behind the universe, and not merely a search for improved technologies, then **nothing can be more scientific than self-enquiry. As with true science, it is the quest for the reality underlying the universe, but it involves an approach that is diametrically opposite to that adopted in Western science.** Self-enquiry employs inward looking awareness as its instrument in contrast to Western science, which employs outward looking awareness. It is an interesting fact of history and a testimony to the enduring truth of most Eastern religious philosophies that, after the lapse of several centuries and the expenditure of astronomical sums of money, the modern scientific worldview is moving towards that held for centuries by the mystics of both the East and the West!

Western science originated during the sixth century B.C. in the Greek culture of the time, where science, philosophy and religion were not separated. The aim of the thinkers of the time was to discover the essential nature or 'physis', of all things, and it led them to a mystical view of the world. All forms of existence were seen as manifestations of a living unity. They even saw no distinction between the inanimate and inanimate, spirit and matter. *The concept of a division between spirit and matter was a subsequent development, leading gradually to a split between philosophy, which dealt with the realm of mind and spirit, and science, which dealt with matter.*

The birth of modern Western science was preceded by an extreme formulation of this spirit - matter dualism by Descartes, in the seventeenth century. The 'Cartesian' division allowed scientists to treat matter as dead and completely separate from themselves, and to develop a mechanistic view of the material world. From the second half of the seventeenth century to the end of the nineteenth century, this mechanistic model of the universe dominated all scientific thought. It flourished alongside philosophies and religions that regarded the universe as subject to the divine law of a monarchical God. **The recent advances made in physics are however now leading science back to the essentially mystical worldview that was held in Western cultures over 2500 years ago.** All this time however, this mystical worldview remained unchanged in Eastern spiritual and scientific traditions, when Western scientific thought had turned away from it.

The technique of self-enquiry provides serious seekers of truth and those seeking a meaningful purpose in life the opportunity to achieve these aims. The Cartesian dictum 'I think, therefore

I exist' led Westerners to equate their identity with their mind instead of their whole organism. As a consequence, *most individuals regard themselves as isolated egos existing within their physical bodies. Advaita philosophy however postulates that all that exists is an indivisible unity.* All things and events perceived by the senses are inter-related, connected and merely different aspects or manifestations of the same ultimate reality. *Science has come round to accepting this view,* - held by almost all Eastern religious philosophies - as it alone provides an adequate philosophical basis for its new theories on the nature of reality. **The seeker after truth is therefore being both scientific and modern when he accepts the philosophy of Advaita and chooses the path of self-enquiry that is based thereon.**

Self-enquiry leads to abidance in the Self or pure Being-Awareness. It is one's true and natural state. According to the mystics, who alone have actually experienced this state, it is also one of bliss or unconditioned happiness and perfect peace. *Our true nature is unalloyed happiness and peace, but we do not feel it to be so. We feel that happiness is derived from external objects and the satisfaction of desires. Everyone seeks absolute and permanent happiness outside oneself, in the belief that it is something to be acquired, whereas it is within oneself as one's very nature.* According to Advaita, this is because one has limited and identified one's true self - the infinite 'I' - with the 'I' thought or sense of individual existence. One has only to end this false identification for one's true nature as unalloyed happiness to manifest.

"One is always the Self, of the nature of bliss. It is the ego that interposes itself between that bliss and the non-bliss of the waking state If one seeks its source, it disappears and the Self or Bliss remains." (Talks. Number 106)

"O mind! You wander far in search of happiness, not knowing your natural state of Freedom. Your home of infinite bliss you

will regain if only you go back the way you came." (Guru Vachaka Kovai Saying 783)

"One's nature is happiness but it is not felt to be so because one has identified one's true self with the ego or false 'I' and the body. If the wrong identification ceases, happiness will manifest." (Talks. Number 295)

"Knowing well that bliss serene is found in Being - the Self - alone, and not in this illusory life, seek and attain the final heaven of grace, the state of 'mouna' (silence), pure Awareness." (Guru Vachaka Kovai Saying 238)

"If happiness comes from possessions, then happiness must be in proportion to one's possessions. And if one is devoid of possessions, one's happiness should be nil. This is not the human experience Happiness must therefore be inherent in man and not due to external causes. If one realizes one's Self, he opens the store of unalloyed happiness (since happiness is the very nature of the Self)." (Talks. Number 3)

"The food we eat eats us. Those who know not this truth, desire and eagerly enjoy earthly pleasures, thinking that they eat it. While in truth, they are being eaten by it." (Guru Vachaka Kovai Saying 591)

"Like one who takes a crocodile for a boat and with its help tries to cross a river, are those who - while they pamper the trivial flesh - claim also that they are earnest seekers of the (bliss of) the living Self." (Guru Vachaka Kovai Saying 125)

"Those who desire, live and love the trivial life the ego knows reject, as if it were unreal, the natural life of infinite bliss within their own hearts - ever present for their enjoyment." (Guru Vachaka Kovai Saying 127)

"Happiness is inherent in the Self. In moments of happiness, one is really diving within into the pure Self, but through

association of ideas one ascribes the happiness to external things or happenings. On these occasions, one is plunging into the Self, though unconsciously. To do so consciously is realization of the Self." (Talks. Number 254)

"The desire for happiness is itself a proof for the ever-existing happiness of our true nature as the Self. The desire for happiness that arises in us is really our seeking our natural state (just as we seek health when we fall sick). The moments of happiness in the waking state are due to the fact that on these occasions, one thought (the pure 'I' thought) excludes all others and then this also merges into the Self." (Talks. Number 619)

"The perfection and natural state of happiness of the pure ego is broken when desire arises. When that desire is fulfilled, the original perfection is restored and the ego is happy. When the ego merges into its source - the Self - in Self-realization, relative, temporary pleasures are transcended and there is perfect peace or bliss, since that is the nature of the Self." (Talks Number 28)

"One who lives in Brahman, the Self or pure 'I' - the sole reality that is of the nature of Existence-Consciousness-Bliss - finds permanent happiness, since happiness is Its very nature. Such a one will not look for other sources of (transitory) happiness. Emergence from the Self is the cause of all unhappiness." (Talks Number 17)

"The desire for permanent happiness and peace bespeaks such permanency of happiness and peace as being our true nature. They are therefore to be gained by regaining our true nature or the state of the Self. The intellect should therefore be turned inwards to seek the true Self within. A stage is finally reached where the intellect ceases to function, as it cannot reach the Self or Higher Power that enabled it to function. Then the Supreme Power alone remains. It is realization of the Self. Being a state of bliss, all desires are then fulfilled." (Talks. Number 502)

"One's nature - being happiness itself - can never be lost, so it is merely re-discovered. The happiness arising from external sources is transient. It is therefore better to seek one's Self and abide therein than seek happiness outside oneself." (Talks. Number 523)

"Look not for God's grace only in the worldly wealth that virtue brings. This grace is present even more in the tranquil clarity of awareness free from all cares, whose cause is but forgetfulness of the Self." (Guru Vachaka Kovai Saying 753)

"Our essential nature - the Self - is happiness, not the mind But we have forgotten our true nature and identify with the mind. We thus experience pleasure and pain, which are merely modes of the mind." (Talks. Number 540)

"Our natural state is one of happiness It is the thoughts that arise in the wake of the 'I' thought in the waking state that hide this inherent happiness. In sleep, there are no thoughts and so one experiences the happiness of the natural state." (Talks. Number 321)

"Unhappiness results from objects If they cease to be, there will be no contingent thoughts to cause unhappiness. One must therefore seek to realize the truth that they are only mental creations, with no substantive being - being present only in the subjective consciousness. The only reality will then be seen to be the Self, permeating and enveloping the world In the absence of duality, no thoughts will arise to disturb the peace of the Self. This is called realization of the Self." (Talks. Number 485)

"Being is, by its nature, Bliss supreme. It is the fickle mind's fond, eager search all day for pleasure in alien objects that ensures the loss of our inherent bliss." (Guru Vachaka Kovai Saying 1026)

"Having found that Self-relish is the highest bliss, the wise abide as Self alone. But those who know not that the sole, certain bliss supreme is in the Self alone, they stay for ever worldly minded." (Guru Vachaka Kovai Saying 1027)

"If, without wasting time, one starts and keeps up steady self-enquiry, one's life becomes at once ennobled; one is no more this suffering body, and there wells up within one's heart a sea of bliss supreme." (Guru Vachaka Kovai Saying 755)

"There is a Unity that runs through the diversity (that one perceives) in the world. It is the Self, which is the same in all. There is no difference in the Self. All the differences we perceive are external or superficial. One can realize the Unity behind all the perceived differences, arrive at a state where distinctions and suffering are not perceived and thus be happy. It is futile to try to find happiness by reforming the world." (Talks. Number 507)

"One wonders why they plough with thought and toil so hard to cultivate the treacherous field of sense, hankering for a tiny grain of pleasure – neglecting the Heart whence thought arises; the nursery ready to reward with plenty a little labour of love." (Guru Vackaka Kovai saying 72)

"What does one gain, you may well ask, by giving up the wealth immense of worldly pleasures and seeking only mere Awareness? The benefit of true Awareness is the unbroken prevalence of peace within the heart, the bliss of one's own natural being." (Guru Vachaka Kovai saying 77)

The gross physical realm in which we live and move is an appearance of, and in, a subtle underlying realm that is of the nature of an energy dance. The subtle is the essence and basis of the material. **The differentiated matter of the material world is a superficial expression of the non-dual spirit that is the sole and fundamental Reality. It is therefore logical that our lives at the materialist level should be based on a**

foundation of spirituality. This has always been the position of all religions. Science now provides this view with scientific validity - since its most recent discoveries have forced it to abandon its earlier philosophical basis that matter and spirit are separate. *The spiritual basis for guiding us in our daily living should however be the direct teachings of the mystics - both Eastern and Western - about the nature of the Reality, and not the lesser man made philosophies, doctrines and moral codes, all of which are mere formulations to suit the diverse temperaments and environments of their followers.*

REFERENCES

1. W. Heisenberg, *Physics and Philosophy* (Allen and Unwin, London, 1963) p. 96

2. D. Bohm and B. Hiley, *On the Intuitive Understanding of Non-locality as Implied by Quantum Theory in* Foundations of Physics Vol. 5. 1975

3. F. Hoyle, *Nature of the Universe* (Penguin Books, London, 1965) p. 124

4. Swami Vivekananda, in *Complete Works of Swami Vivekananda* Vol. 3. p. 26

5. M. Kroy, *The Divinization of Science. Paper submitted to the International Conference on Science and Spirituality, Rome. October 1983*

6. G. Zukov, *An Overview of Physics* (Fontana 1982) p. 115

7. E. Schrodinger, *What is Life?* in Science and Spirituality, (Sathya Sai Trust, Bombay 1985) p. 156

8. D.T. Suzuki, in Preface to *Mahayana Buddhism* (Allen and Unwin, London, 1959) p. 33

9. F. Capra, *The Tao of Physics* (Flamingo, London, 1982) p. 189

10. L. de Broglie, in P.A. Schilpp, *Albert Einstein – Philosopher Scientist* (Library of Living Philosophers, Evanston, Illinois, 1949) p. 114

11. Roger Jones, *Physics as a Metaphor* (Abacus 1983) p. 139

12. G. Zukov, *An Overview of Physics* (Fontana 1982) p. 172

13. S. Radhakrishnan, *Indian Philosophy* (Allen and Unwin. London 1951) p. 530

14. Swami Vivekananda, *Jnana Yoga* (Advaita Ashram, Calcutta, 1972) p. 109

15. Swami Vivekananda, *Complete Works of Vivekananda,* Part 1. p. 95

16. James Jeans, *The Mysterious Universe* (Longman, London 1930) p. 94

17. A. de Reinecourt, *The Third Eye* (W. Morrow and Co. N.Y. 1981)

18. S. Radhakrishnan, *Indian Philosophy* (Allen and Unwin, London 1951) p. 557

19. Sri Aurobindo, *Synthesis of Yoga* (Aurobindo Ashram, Pondicherry 1957) p. 989

20. A. Einstein, in M. Capek, *The Philosophical Impact of Contemporary Physics* (Princeton, N.J. 1961) p. 317 – 319

21. W. Thirring, in Capra, *The Tao of Physics* (Flamingo, London, 1982) p. 246

22. Fung Yu-Lan, *Short History of Chinese Philosophy* (Macmillan N.Y. 1958) p. 279

23. S. Radhakrishnan, *Indian Philosophy* (Allen and Unwin, London 1951) p. 550

24. F. Capra, *The Tao of Physics* (Flamingo, London, 1982) p. 275

25. Ibid., p. 290

26. Ibid., p. 296

27. Ibid., p. 303

28. Ibid., p. 305

29. S. Radhakrishnan, *Indian Philosophy* (Allen and Unwin, London, 1951) p. 369

30. F. Capra, *The Tao of Physics* (Flamingo, London, 1982) p. 353

31. Ibid., p. 316

32. Ibid., p. 326

33. Ibid., p. 326

34. G.F. Chew, *Bootstrap – A Scientific Idea in Science*, Vol. 161. p. 762

35. James Jeans, *The Mysterious Universe* (Longman, London 1930) p. 2-3

36. A. Einstein, in Lincoln Barnett, *The Universe and Dr. Einstein* quoted in *Science and Spirituality* (Sathya Sai Trust, Bombay) p. 112

37. Mark Abrams, *Albert Einstein* in *Sanathana Sarathi, May 1992* (Sathya Sai Publication)

38. H. Pattie, in *Science and Spirituality* (Sathya Sai Trust, Bombay 1985) p. 95

39. James Jeans, in *Science and Spirituality* (Sathya Sai Trust, Bombay, 19855) p. 79

40. G.F. Chew, *Bootstrap – A Scientific Idea in Science*, Vol. 161. p. 763

41. S. Grof, *Realms of the Human Unconscious* (Dutton N.Y. 1976)

42. E. Jantsch, The Self Organizing Universe (Pergamon N.Y. 1984) p. 308

43. C. Jung, in Science and Spirituality (Sathya Sai Book Trust) p. 186

44. A. Einstein, in Science and Spirituality (Sathya Sai Book Trust) p. 151

45. F. Capra, Tao of Physics (Flamingo, London 1982) p. 358

RECOMMENDED READING

G. Bateson, *Mind and Nature* (Wildwood House, London 1979)

N. Bohr, *Atomic Physics and Human Knowledge* (John Wiley and Sons. N.Y. 1858)

M. Capek, *The Philosophical Impact of Contemporary Physics* (D von Nostrand, Princeton, N.J. 1961)

F. Capra, *The Tao of Physics* (Flamingo, London 1982)

F. Capra, *The Turning Point* (Flamingo, London, 1983)

S. Grof, *Realms of the Human Unconscious* (Souvenir Press, London 1979)

W. Heisenberg, *Physics and Philosophy* (Allen and Unwin, London 1963)

W. Heisenberg, *Physics and Beyond* (Allen and Unwin, London 1971)

W. James, *The Varieties of Religious Experience* (Fontana, London 1971)

R.D. Laing, *The Voice of Experience* (Pantheon, N.Y. 1982)

K. Lakshmana Sarma, *Maha Yoga* (Sri Ramanasramam, Tiruvannamalai, S. India)

E. Laszlo, *The Systems View of the World* (Braziller, N.Y. 1972)

J.E. Lovelock, *Gaia* (Oxford University Press, 1979)

T.M.P. Mahadevan, *Ramana Maharshi and His Philosophy of Existence* (Sri Ramanasramam, Tiruvannamalai, S. India, 1959)

Sri Muruganar, *The Garland of Guru's Sayings - Translated from the Tamil by Prof. K. Swaminathan* (Sri Ramanasramam, Tiruvannamalai, S. India)

S. Radhakrishnan, *Indian Philosophy* (Allen and Unwin, London 1951)

P.A. Schilpp, *Einstein; Philosopher-Scientist* (Tudor, N.Y. 1951)

Sri Ramanasramam, *Talks with Sri Ramana Maharshi* (Sri Ramanasramam, Tiruvannamalai, 1955)

D.R. Suzuki, *The Essence of Buddhism* (Hozokan, Kyoto, Japan 1968)

S. Vivekananda, *Jnana Yoga* (Advaita Ashram, Calcutta, 1972)

INDEX

A

Absolute, 10, 33, 36, 41, 42, 45, 61, 68, 73, 74, 76, 85, 97, 112, 134, 137, 140, 143, 145, 157, 170
adhyasa, 127
Advaita Vedanta, 4, 29, 32, 33, 36, 41, 45, 67, 84, 85, 89, 94, 97, 99, 110, 127, 135, 140, 143, 144, 155, 170, 183, 189, 190
aham, 185, 186
ahamvritti, 185
ajata doctrine, 55
ajnani, 34, 74, 111, 157, 189
akasa, 82, 93, 121
alpha particles, 22
Arjuna, 110
astrophysics, 22, 149
atom, 22, 24, 40, 99, 135
    atomic nucleus, 25
    atomic orbit, 24
    atomic physics, 22, 23, 43, 48, 52, 90, 97, 118
Auvaiyar, 16
AvatatamsakaSutra, 4
avidya, 33, 36, 74, 84, 85, 110, 127, 128
Awareness, 41, 42, 46, 58, 69, 71, 72, 73, 75, 80, 83, 89, 93, 96, 114, 127, 128, 129, 130, 133, 135, 151, 154, 157, 172, 173, 175, 186, 187, 188, 189, 192, 196
    pure, 35, 45, 47, 74, 83, 129, 174, 175, 193

B

Bateson, 150, 151, 201

becoming, 79, 87, 89, 94, 107, 143, 181
Being, 5, 8, 31, 32, 33, 34, 35, 37, 38, 41, 42, 46, 47, 48, 51, 53, 59, 60, 69, 71, 72, 73, 74, 75, 76, 78, 79, 80, 83, 94, 95, 96, 107, 108, 109, 112, 120, 130, 131, 132, 134, 136, 140, 144, 145, 164, 178, 180, 184, 185, 186, 189, 193, 194, 195
    Awareness, 8, 35, 69, 78, 96, 120, 134, 178, 180, 185
    Awareness-Bliss, 78, 96, 180, 185
    formless, 41, 42
    pure, 157, 192
    real, 131
    Supreme, 81, 85
Bhagavad Gita, 49, 84, 110, 160
bhava
    ananya, 183, 184, 185
    anya, 183
Bliss, 9, 15, 96, 192, 194, 195
body, 145
    material, 76
    subtle, 76, 111, 173, 174
Bohm, 122, 123, 198
Bootstrap, 124, 200
Brahman, 29, 30, 31, 32, 33, 36, 38, 41, 47, 48, 53, 54, 59, 67, 69, 73, 74, 78, 79, 80, 81, 84, 85, 92, 96, 97, 98, 111, 116, 127, 132, 134, 135, 139, 140, 143, 144, 145, 146, 154, 156, 157, 169, 170, 186, 194
Buddha, 171
Buddhism, Mahayana, 4, 136, 198

C

Capra, 151, 198, 199, 200, 201

Cartesian, 7, 24, 149, 150, 166, 167, 191
cause, 67, 79, 123, 141, 142
   causation, causality, 3, 32, 67, 68, 84, 95, 97
   material, 31, 80
Chew, 123, 124, 139, 200
chidvyoman, 177
Christ, 8, 9, 10, 11
Consciousness, 3, 9, 11, 29, 30, 31, 44, 45, 49, 54, 70, 71, 72, 73, 80, 82, 83, 95, 96, 97, 106, 109, 112, 127, 128, 131, 134, 139, 140, 144, 145, 146, 148, 150, 151, 155, 156, 157, 158, 168, 169, 171, 173, 174, 176, 177, 182, 184, 188, 194
   Absolute, 45, 76, 137, 140, 145, 157
   Cosmic, 44, 82, 95, 143, 145, 146, 169
   Pure, 9, 38, 45, 47, 78, 81, 108, 109, 121, 143, 144, 145, 177, 181, 182
cosmology, 22, 40, 149
cosmos, 40, 47, 80, 82, 87, 100, 122, 140, 145, 155, 157, 168
   cosmic consciousness, 140, 141, 145, 149
   cosmic dance, 82, 98, 99, 120
   cosmic law, 113
creation, 10, 45, 47, 49, 65, 71, 79, 80, 81, 82, 83, 88, 95, 97, 98, 99, 100, 104, 107, 122, 140, 143, 146

D

Darwin, 142
Descartes, 17, 19, 191
determinism, 19
Devi Bhagavata, 83
devotion, 10, 42, 75, 160, 184, 185
dimensional, 3, 18, 21, 23, 26, 50, 51, 57, 61, 62, 63, 64, 65, 66, 67, 88, 89, 103, 139, 148, 149, 157
   four, 50, 61
   higher, 51
duality, 8, 10, 42, 44, 49, 133, 170, 180, 195
dyads, 49
dynamic, 3, 11, 12, 25, 26, 27, 40, 49, 50, 51, 52, 63, 64, 78, 82, 83, 86, 87, 88, 89, 92, 93, 94, 95, 97, 101, 102, 103, 104, 105, 113, 120, 122, 123, 124, 136, 138, 151, 154, 159, 160, 164
   pattern, 25, 26, 51, 88, 89, 94, 97
   process, 40
   unity, 50, 52, 94
   web, 26, 27, 40, 86, 123, 124

E

ecology, 14, 167
   ecological awareness, 167, 168
ego, 9, 10, 31, 35, 41, 42, 44, 46, 47, 49, 55, 56, 57, 58, 69, 71, 72, 73, 74, 75, 76, 77, 78, 81, 95, 107, 108, 113, 114, 115, 130, 133, 135, 145, 150, 161, 163, 170, 171, 172, 173, 174, 175, 176, 177, 178, 179, 180, 181, 182, 184, 185, 186, 187, 188, 192, 193, 194
Einstein, 20, 21, 60, 61, 63, 91, 92, 118, 142, 198, 199, 200, 201
electrodynamics, 20, 91
electromagnetism, 19
electron, 24, 25, 119
   waves, 24, 25
energy, 2, 21, 22, 24, 25, 26, 27, 40, 82, 83, 84, 87, 88, 89, 92, 93, 97, 98, 99, 101, 103, 104, 105, 120, 124, 135, 146, 148, 149, 154, 169, 196

Index

kinetic, 88, 98
energy bundles, 88
energy dance, 99, 196
EPR experiment, 119, 122
eternal now, 64
ether, 54, 96, 121, 122
  physical, 54, 122
  transcendental, 54
Euclidean, 18, 57
evolution, 79, 87, 142, 143, 146, 151, 166
Existence, 3, 9, 29, 30, 52, 58, 68, 69, 70, 127, 154, 155, 157, 170, 172, 173, 174, 184, 194, 201
experience, 4, 7, 8, 17, 18, 21, 25, 27, 31, 35, 36, 37, 39, 41, 44, 51, 53, 55, 56, 57, 60, 61, 62, 63, 64, 66, 67, 69, 71, 72, 73, 74, 75, 76, 83, 84, 85, 97, 98, 106, 108, 113, 115, 118, 127, 131, 132, 133, 136, 141, 142, 144, 145, 147, 148, 149, 153, 155, 156, 157, 158, 159, 164, 165, 175, 179, 186, 187, 188, 189, 193, 195
  perinatal, 147
  psychedelic, 147, 148, 149
  psychodynamic, 147
  trans-personal, 147
Eye, 38, 75, 199
  real, 72

F

Faraday, 19
field, 3, 19, 50, 66, 82, 91, 92, 93, 94, 95, 99, 105, 122, 130, 190, 196
  theory, 66, 95, 99
force, 3, 13, 18, 19, 20, 25, 26, 27, 50, 52, 91, 94, 140
  nuclear, 25, 86
force field, 19, 20
form, 10, 12, 20, 21, 22, 23, 24, 25, 27, 29, 32, 37, 42, 52, 61, 71, 72, 73, 78, 82, 86, 87, 88, 89, 91, 93, 94, 101, 104, 105, 108, 109, 113, 114, 121, 122, 126, 133, 134, 138, 146, 162, 164, 167, 169, 172, 173, 174, 179, 183, 185, 187

G

Gaia, 150, 201
galaxies, 79, 87, 152
Gandhi, Mahatma, 161
Gaudapada, 67
God, 10, 16, 17, 37, 41, 42, 45, 53, 72, 75, 109, 114, 152, 160, 161, 163, 164, 167, 170, 171, 172, 179, 181, 183, 184, 185, 191, 195
gravity, 18, 19, 21, 63, 64, 87, 91
  gravitational field, 21, 63, 91
Great Doer, 14
Grof, 147, 200, 201

H

hadron, 101, 104, 105, 136, 138, 139, 146
happiness, 14, 113, 163, 192, 193, 194, 195, 196
harmony, 1, 8, 11, 12, 13, 14, 80, 81, 111, 125, 140, 153, 156, 159, 164, 190
Heart, 44, 54, 55, 73, 171, 175, 177, 184, 196
Heisenberg, 103, 198, 201
Hellenic, 102
Higher Power, 116, 161, 194
Hinduism, 27, 41, 62, 82, 86, 98, 168, 169
holomovement, 122, 123
humanism, 11

I

I AM, 42, 74, 79, 135, 140, 186

idam, 186
ignorance, 10, 31, 33, 35, 41, 71, 74, 77, 120, 127, 128, 129, 133, 188
illusion, 5, 11, 24, 33, 36, 46, 57, 58, 66, 67, 93, 96, 97, 110, 112, 131, 147, 148, 174, 185
implicate order, 122, 123
inertia, 87
intellect, 32, 33, 37, 38, 67, 76, 77, 85, 130, 131, 132, 136, 141, 156, 157, 158, 164, 189, 194
intelligence, 15, 72, 80, 81, 140, 143, 154, 170
interpenetration, 136, 138
intuition, 12, 141, 158, 159, 166

J

jagratsushupti, 52, 136
Jesus, 16
jiva, 45, 122, 171, 175, 178
jivatma, 140
jnana, 163
jnani, 34, 111, 120, 130, 157, 189

K

Kabir, 135
kalpa, 87
karma, 113, 114, 115, 116, 126, 162
Kathopanishad, 82
Kingdom of God, 15
knower, 29, 37, 44, 46, 51, 127, 128, 130, 133
knowledge, 3, 6, 29, 30, 33, 36, 37, 38, 39, 41, 44, 46, 49, 51, 52, 66, 68, 69, 73, 74, 75, 85, 103, 105, 119, 127, 128, 129, 130, 131, 132, 133, 134, 136, 141, 142, 149, 153, 155, 156, 158, 159, 164, 165, 166, 169, 188, 189
absolute, 33, 38, 49, 51, 112, 127, 132
indirect, 132
objective, 48, 128, 129, 130, 149, 155
perfect, 36, 119, 130
pure, 37, 128, 133
relative, 37, 38, 49, 51, 127, 129, 130, 131, 132, 133, 134
Krishna, 110

L

Liberation, 15, 16, 76, 131
Light, 38, 52, 77, 134, 155
lila, 82, 87
Lord, 30, 41, 98, 110, 115, 134, 163, 164, 171

M

magnetic, 19, 52, 91
  field, 52, 91
  force, 19
  phenomena, 19
Mahayana Buddhism, 4, 136, 198
mass, 13, 18, 21, 23, 24, 25, 27, 63, 65, 87, 88, 101, 124
matter, 3, 17, 18, 21, 22, 23, 24, 25, 26, 27, 29, 36, 50, 52, 64, 79, 81, 82, 86, 88, 89, 91, 92, 93, 94, 95, 97, 98, 99, 100, 113, 117, 121, 122, 123, 124, 125, 130, 135, 142, 143, 146, 148, 149, 150, 151, 154, 157, 165, 169, 174, 191, 196
Max Planck equation, 135
Maxwell, 19, 20
mechanical, 2, 19, 24, 166
  stability, 24
  system, 2, 19, 166
mechanics, 19, 20
mechanistic world view, 21
meditation, 45, 74, 117, 156, 161, 177, 180, 181, 182, 183, 184, 190

Index

mind, 3, 4, 5, 6, 8, 10, 17, 32, 33, 34, 37, 38, 39, 44, 45, 46, 47, 51, 53, 54, 55, 56, 57, 59, 60, 61, 63, 66, 68, 70, 71, 72, 73, 74, 75, 76, 77, 78, 80, 81, 83, 85, 87, 96, 97, 102, 106, 107, 108, 109, 110, 111, 112, 116, 121, 122, 125, 131, 132, 133, 134, 135, 138, 139, 140, 142, 147, 150, 151, 152, 156, 158, 160, 164, 167, 171, 172, 173, 174, 175, 176, 177, 178, 180, 181, 182, 183, 184, 185, 186, 187, 189, 191, 192, 195
mind ether, 54, 122
mouna, 193
mystic experience, 6, 33, 36, 40, 41, 44, 48, 94, 136, 160, 169
mystic state, 39
mysticism, 4, 12, 43, 48, 50, 53, 63, 69, 94, 117, 131, 142, 146, 153, 154, 155, 156, 157, 158, 159, 164, 167

N

Nature, 6, 11, 17, 84, 124, 127, 139, 144, 150, 165, 198, 201
Newtonian, 17, 18, 19, 20, 94, 149
   laws of motion, 19
   mechanics, 17, 20
   model, 18, 19
   physics, 19
   world view, 20
nirguna, 79
   Brahman, 79
non-action, 164
nucleon, 95

O

objects, 8, 32, 33, 34, 38, 39, 47, 48, 51, 54, 55, 57, 58, 62, 81, 82, 83, 86, 88, 89, 93, 94, 95, 96, 97, 103, 111, 112, 117, 118, 121, 122, 124, 128, 129, 130, 134, 136, 145, 149, 157, 178, 187, 192, 195
One, the, 10
Opposites, 48, 50
   polar, 50
oscillation, 20, 50, 62

P

paradox, 23, 103
Paramatma, 140
particle, 25, 26, 65, 67, 103
   sub-atomic, 17, 23, 36, 86, 88, 90, 94, 97, 98, 99, 101, 103, 112, 152
   virtual, 95, 99
particle exchange, 94, 118
particle world, 26, 27, 95, 102, 117
pattern, 26, 52, 53
   dynamic, 25, 26, 51, 88, 89, 94, 97
   energy, 3, 26, 27, 40, 88, 98, 99, 101, 120, 148, 149
perception, 3, 17, 46, 52, 59, 68, 73, 76, 85, 97, 111, 131, 134, 141, 144, 147, 148, 149, 150, 166, 167, 168, 170, 172, 176, 180, 187, 189
perfection, 11, 51, 52, 82, 142, 194
philosophy, 1, 2, 4, 5, 6, 7, 8, 9, 10, 13, 14, 17, 29, 35, 84, 85, 102, 106, 124, 125, 134, 135, 140, 144, 153, 159, 160, 161, 166, 168, 169, 171, 183, 189, 190, 191, 192
   Western, 2, 89
photon, 24, 65
physics, 2, 9, 20, 26, 27, 28, 36, 40, 41, 43, 46, 50, 51, 53, 57, 79, 80, 82, 86, 87, 92, 93, 95, 97, 98, 99, 102, 117, 118, 122, 124, 146, 154, 155, 169, 191
   classical, 2, 3, 17, 20, 21, 22,

23, 39, 87, 95, 105, 118, 139, 144, 153, 154
experimental, 17
modern, 2, 3, 14, 18, 35, 40, 45, 53, 60, 63, 66, 80, 82, 86, 89, 94, 100, 101, 124, 125, 132, 144, 153, 160, 172
particle, 102, 137, 139
relativistic, 50, 51, 62, 65, 66
physis, 2, 191
prajna, 141
prana, 82, 140
Prigogine, 151

Q

quanta, 23, 52, 91
Quantum, 22, 23, 24, 39, 41, 65, 89, 94, 117, 154, 198
electrodynamics, 20, 91
field, 65, 94
theory, 23, 24, 39, 41, 89, 154
quark, 102, 120, 121, 138
model, 102, 120
pattern, 121
structure, 120, 121, 138

R

radiation, 22, 24, 27, 52, 91, 98
Reality, 7, 8, 29, 30, 31, 32, 33, 34, 35, 38, 39, 41, 42, 44, 47, 48, 49, 51, 53, 56, 58, 59, 61, 64, 67, 69, 70, 71, 72, 73, 75, 76, 77, 78, 79, 80, 83, 84, 85, 89, 92, 93, 97, 106, 110, 112, 114, 115, 117, 119, 127, 128, 131, 133, 134, 136, 139, 144, 154, 155, 156, 157, 158, 160, 161, 163, 169, 170, 171, 172, 173, 175, 179, 182, 185, 188, 196
Realization, 51, 52, 132, 133, 186, 188
Relativity, 20, 25, 43, 61, 62, 88, 89
Rutherford, 22

S

sadhana, 156, 180
samadhi, 39, 51, 75, 76
nirvikalpa, 73
sahaja, 62, 136, 139
samsara, 84
Sankara, 4, 31, 67, 85, 143, 144
sannyasi, 163
Satan, 10, 175
Self, 8, 15, 29, 30, 31, 32, 34, 35, 36, 37, 38, 39, 41, 44, 45, 47, 48, 49, 51, 52, 54, 55, 56, 58, 59, 60, 69, 71, 72, 73, 74, 75, 76, 77, 78, 79, 80, 93, 96, 107, 108, 109, 110, 111, 113, 114, 115, 116, 117, 119, 121, 122, 126, 128, 129, 130, 131, 132, 133, 134, 135, 136, 144, 145, 157, 160, 161, 162, 163, 164, 171, 172, 174, 175, 176, 177, 178, 179, 180, 182, 183, 184, 185, 186, 187, 188, 189, 190, 192, 193, 194, 195, 196, 200
Awareness, 79, 80
enquiry, 160
Self Awareness, 79, 80
self organization, 151
sensations, 43, 71, 147
sense perception, 39, 140, 141
senses, 29, 32, 33, 38, 39, 44, 51, 53, 55, 61, 62, 68, 71, 73, 75, 83, 85, 97, 108, 112, 131, 132, 139, 157, 162, 172, 192
Shakti, 83
Shiva, 83, 98, 100
dance of, 82, 98, 100, 164
singularities, 104
Siva, 31, 45, 83, 161
solar system, 19
space, 3, 18, 19, 20, 21, 22, 23, 24, 27, 32, 33, 40, 47, 50, 51, 52, 54, 57, 58, 59, 60, 61, 62,

Index

63, 64, 65, 66, 67, 68, 69, 70, 72, 73, 74, 80, 81, 85, 86, 87, 88, 89, 91, 92, 93, 94, 95, 96, 97, 98, 103, 119, 120, 121, 122, 132, 136, 139, 144, 148, 149
physical, 54, 121
space-time, 21, 27, 33, 50, 51, 52, 61, 62, 63, 64, 65, 66, 67, 88, 89, 103, 139
continuum, 27, 61, 66
diagram, 65
spirit, 8, 17, 29, 30, 81, 96, 157, 160, 166, 168, 191, 196
spirit-matter dualism, 17
state, 11, 12, 15, 24, 32, 36, 37, 43, 44, 45, 46, 51, 52, 53, 55, 57, 59, 60, 62, 63, 64, 74, 75, 76, 77, 79, 85, 89, 90, 93, 95, 99, 103, 106, 107, 109, 111, 112, 114, 129, 131, 136, 137, 138, 139, 146, 149, 153, 154, 155, 156, 163, 164, 166, 170, 172, 173, 175, 176, 178, 180, 183, 184, 185, 186, 187, 188, 189, 192, 193, 194, 195, 196
dream, 108, 111
natural, 74, 108, 175, 177, 192, 194, 195
sleep, 57, 76, 109
waking, 35, 46, 47, 52, 59, 76, 77, 106, 107, 108, 109, 111, 112, 116, 133, 136, 174, 176, 186, 192, 194, 195
sub-atomic, 17, 22, 23, 26, 27, 36, 46, 50, 52, 60, 65, 80, 82, 86, 88, 89, 90, 94, 97, 98, 99, 100, 101, 103, 112, 117, 136, 146, 150, 152
sub-atomic level, 23
sunya, 45, 137
surrender, 9, 10, 42, 116, 161
symmetry, 65, 102
systems theory, 12, 151

T

Tao, 169, 198, 199, 200, 201
theobserved, 18, 21, 43, 44, 45, 80, 104, 105, 106, 120, 123
theobserver, 3, 19, 24, 27, 43, 44, 45, 60, 61, 80, 104, 107, 146, 154, 172
theocentric, 11
time, 1, 3, 11, 18, 20, 21, 23, 24, 26, 27, 31, 32, 51, 52, 53, 57, 58, 59, 60, 61, 62, 63, 64, 65, 66, 67, 68, 69, 70, 73, 79, 80, 81, 85, 86, 87, 88, 90, 95, 97, 119, 120, 122, 123, 124, 132, 135, 136, 139, 144, 148, 149, 159, 179, 187, 189, 191, 196
triad, 111, 120
triputi, 45
Truth, 8, 36, 37, 38, 47, 49, 110, 127, 130, 132

U

unity, 1, 2, 3, 11, 12, 26, 29, 30, 31, 33, 35, 36, 38, 40, 42, 44, 48, 50, 52, 55, 69, 72, 85, 96, 97, 112, 119, 120, 127, 136, 151, 156, 167, 172, 191, 192
dynamic, 50, 52, 94
unity of opposites, 49
universe, 2, 4, 5, 6, 7, 8, 9, 11, 12, 14, 18, 19, 21, 22, 23, 26, 27, 29, 33, 34, 36, 39, 40, 41, 43, 44, 45, 47, 48, 50, 54, 61, 64, 67, 68, 69, 78, 79, 80, 81, 82, 83, 84, 85, 86, 87, 89, 95, 96, 97, 98, 99, 118, 119, 120, 122, 123, 124, 126, 132, 133, 135, 136, 138, 140, 141, 142, 143, 144, 145, 146, 148, 149, 150, 152, 153, 154, 155, 157, 164, 166, 169, 177, 190, 191
participatory, 43, 45, 80
Upanishads, 3, 5, 78, 132, 135

V

vasanas, 187, 189
Vedas, 4, 79, 80, 81, 82, 84, 131, 139, 140, 142, 143, 144
  Vedic philosophy, 40, 78, 82, 83, 95, 96, 106
velocity, 60
vichara, 75
vidya, 127
Vishnu, 109
Vivekananda, 40, 110, 198, 199, 202
void, 3, 45, 73, 80, 82, 83, 92, 93, 95, 97, 99, 129

W

waves, 20, 22, 23, 50, 52, 86, 91
  probability, 23
  standing, 24
Whole, 36, 56, 175
Will, 82
  Cosmic, 82, 146
  Divine, 160, 161
world, 2, 4, 5, 6, 7, 9, 10, 12, 13, 15, 17, 18, 19, 20, 22, 25, 26, 27, 29, 30, 31, 32, 33, 34, 35, 36, 37, 38, 39, 40, 42, 43, 44, 45, 46, 47, 48, 49, 50, 51, 52, 53, 54, 55, 56, 57, 58, 59, 60, 61, 62, 63, 64, 65, 66, 67, 68, 69, 70, 71, 72, 73, 74, 75, 76, 77, 78, 81, 82, 83, 84, 85, 86, 87, 89, 90, 92, 94, 96, 97, 98, 99, 101, 102, 103, 105, 106, 107, 108, 109, 110, 111, 112, 113, 114, 115, 117, 118, 119, 120, 121, 122, 123, 124, 128, 129, 130, 131, 132, 134, 136, 139, 142, 144, 145, 148, 149, 150, 153, 154, 155, 156, 157, 158, 159, 160, 161, 163, 165, 166, 167, 169, 170, 171, 172, 173, 174, 176, 178, 180, 181, 183, 188, 190, 191, 195, 196
  pluralistic, 32, 48, 69, 85
  world appearance, 4, 31, 33, 34, 35, 38, 54, 58, 69, 71, 72, 78, 82, 96, 99, 112, 119, 121, 153, 174
  world phenomena, 36, 114, 163

Z

Zen Buddhism, 4
Zone of middle dimensions, 21, 27